THE DOCTRINE OF THE TRINITY

THE DOCTRINE OF THE TRINITY

CYRIL C. RICHARDSON

NEW YORK • NASHVILLE
ABINGDON PRESS

THE DOCTRINE OF THE TRINITY

Library of Congress Catalog Card Number: 58-5393

SET UP, PRINTED, AND BOUND BY THE PARTHENON PRESS, AT NASHVILLE, TENNESSEE, UNITED STATES OF AMERICA

Ad uxorem
animam dulcem
miram in specie et castitate
coniugem dulcissimam

PREFACE

I have tried in this book to state as succinctly and clearly as possible the leading doctrines of the Trinity as they have developed in the Church's thought, and to raise some basic questions about their validity. What I have written is in the interests of clarification; and although I feel that none of these doctrines is satisfactory, and all of them involve either confusions of different issues or arbitrary elements, it may well be that my objections can be answered. That I must leave to my critics. I do hope, however, I have sufficiently shown that both ancient and modern views pose more problems than they answer, and often fail to illuminate the basic truths of the Christian gospel. That we must make distinctions in the Godhead, I have constantly stressed; but that these distinctions fall into a neat, threefold pattern is far from apparent. There are distinctions of various kinds to be made, and we cannot sum them up under traditional symbols of Father, Son, and Spirit, which themselves are ambiguous and even overlap. If at least it is felt I have begun to ask the right questions, even though my conclusions may not be acceptable, I shall be satisfied that I have rendered a service.

My colleague, Prof. Daniel Williams, has been kind enough to read my manuscript and to suggest a number of changes I have incorporated. To him I am much indebted. He has, furthermore, raised two most acute criticisms of my book, and I should like to mention them here, since consideration of them does not easily fall within the text as I have written it. Their significance, however, for the reader will naturally be appreciated after, rather than before, reading the text.

The first point is this: Why do I champion a basic self-contradiction in thinking about God (i.e., as Absolute and Related), but criticize contradictions in the classical patterns of trinitarian thinking? Do I not thereby frustrate my own argument? My reply would be that Christian theology is perpetually driven to state apparent contradictions. These are necessary and inevitable. But the clear recognition of these is very different both from attempting to *compose* them by concealed contradictions, and from introducing *arbitrary* ones. What I have tried to do is to show how trinitarian doctrines have often involved contradictions which were not recognized as such, and have admitted arbitrary elements which confuse rather than clarify the real issues.

The second criticism concerns abstract thinking. Why do I condemn the procedure which tries to establish the Trinity by an analysis of abstract thinking, while my own basic distinction in the Godhead (as Absolute and Related) is itself the fruit of such thinking? I should reply that what I question is *not* abstract thinking as such, but the attempt to find the pattern of the Trinity in the *mind as it thinks*. Precisely because the nature of God is paradoxical, the thinking mind does not offer a proper analogy of it. For human thinking and the duality it involves are not paradoxical in the way God's absolute character contrasts with his being in relation. In the former case there is a genuine unity —the mind begets the thought. But in God the distinction is not such. His absolute character does not *generate* his being in relation. He exists in these two ways; and if we try to bring them into relationship, we compromise his absoluteness. We have to state a contradiction for which we can find no analogy in the thinking mind. There are many ways in which my basic distinction in the Godhead can be expressed. We can speak, for instance, of God's essence and his actuality, of his being pure joy and yet participating in suffering, and so on. But in each case a contrast and an inner contradiction are involved, to which the thinking mind affords no possible analogy.

Finally, I must express my thanks to another colleague, Prof. John Knox, who has read the New Testament section and given me helpful advice in several places.

CYRIL C. RICHARDSON

NOTE: While my book was in the press, the illuminating article, "Some Reflections on the Origins of the Doctrine of the Trinity," by Maurice Wiles, appeared in *The Journal of Theological Studies*, April, 1957, pages 92-106. I am encouraged to find another theologian independently raising some of the issues I have tried to treat, and arriving at conclusions not dissimilar to my own.

CONTENTS

CHAPTER I

THE POINT OF VIEW

THE CHRISTIAN DOCTRINE OF THE TRINITY AFFIRMS THAT WHILE God is one, he exists as three persons. "We worship one God in Trinity, and Trinity in Unity," says the so-called Athanasian creed. "There is one Person of the Father, another of the Son, and another of the Holy Ghost." They are all one, coeternal, uncreated, incomprehensible, and almighty. Yet there are three persons, distinguished by the fact that the Father is unbegotten, the Son begotten, and the Spirit proceeding from the Father and (or through) the Son. Is such a doctrine intelligible, and does it either illuminate Christian faith or guard essential truths of our belief?

That is the question to be examined in the following chapters. I shall discuss the historical roots of the doctrine and the leading ways in which it has been interpreted in Christian history. In the course of my argument it will become clear that I wish to enter various objections to the doctrine. It may be well, therefore, to begin with a basic statement of the conclusions from which these chapters have been written. The thesis is this: While it is necessary to make distinctions in the Godhead, these are of various kinds and do not lend themselves to a neat, trinitarian pattern. Different problems and distinctions are involved. Their terms cannot be treated as identical and summed up under the symbols of Father, Son, and Spirit. The historic forms of trinitarian thinking have frequently involved artificialities, partly because different issues have been confused, and partly because the terms "Father," "Son," and "Spirit" are ambiguous, and their meanings tend to overlap. Within the New Testament they signify different things and come from a varied background of religious myth and language. But it is in the "threeness" of the Trinity that the main artificiality lies, and I shall try to show later that the essential meaning of the Trinity in its classical formulations is not necessarily connected with the number three.

Although the theme of this book may therefore seem a negative one, it is only such on the surface. If it can be shown that we can, and ought, to express our Christian belief otherwise, something positive will be accomplished. We shall be able to think more clearly and be unembarrassed by what has often proved a stumbling block to the thoughtful Christian. Furthermore, in examining the New Testament terms and the classical patterns of trinitarian theology, it may be possible to show what *are* the vital concerns of the Christian faith, which the doctrine of the Trinity often beclouds. That, at any rate, is my purpose.

Before, however, I plunge into my argument, it is necessary to make some preliminary points to avoid being misunderstood. First and foremost, it must be stated categorically that the point of view of these chapters is not Unitarian. My purpose is to try to say something which is as relevant to those who hold a very strict, orthodox view of the person of Jesus Christ, as to those who have more liberal persuasions. That it was God himself who was taking action in human history in Jesus of Nazareth, and revealing himself in terms of a human person, is not to be questioned. What is to be questioned is whether the doctrine of the Trinity is a necessary corollary of this, or a cogent and adequate way of speaking of the God who thus manifested himself.

Secondly, it must be emphasized that the objections to be brought against the doctrine of the Trinity do not concern its paradoxical character. The problem, how can three be one and one three, is not an idle problem. Whenever we speak of God we are involved in using paradoxical and apparently contradictory language. The question at issue is not whether we can avoid these dilemmas by some simplified doctrine of God (that, it will be made clear, is impossible). Rather it is whether the Trinity expresses these necessary contradictions adequately. It is my opinion that it confuses them by trying to combine different paradoxes in an artificial threefoldness.

Thirdly, it must be stressed that the concerns which lay behind the rise of the doctrine of the Trinity and which have been variously expressed in the classical interpretations of it, are very *real* concerns. It is not with any desire of minimizing these or regarding them as unimportant, that these chapters are written. Rather the intention is to show that the Trinity does not adequately express them, and confronts the Christian with a doctrine which engenders bewilderment instead of true faith.

Fourthly, it must be recognized that the subject is one of great difficulty. Not only is the literature on it so enormous that scarcely a lifetime would suffice to master it, but also trinitarian doctrine has generated the most subtle speculations which are not easy to follow. It has been observed that while one may be in danger of losing his soul by denying it, he is in equal danger of losing his wits in trying to understand it. The subject, then, must be approached with a good deal of humility. Certainly I may be wrong in my contentions, and it may be possible to state the doctrine of the Trinity in such a way that my objections can be answered. What, therefore, is here written, is written with a view to clarification and not with dogmatic self-assurance. Yet I cannot but think that the doctrine of the Trinity, far from being established, is open to very serious criticism, because of both the modern understanding of the Scriptures, and inherent confusions in its expression.

This leads to the final point. I regard it as axiomatic that the writers of the New Testament were, in one respect, trying to do the same thing we are trying to do, viz., to find appropriate language and symbols by which to express their faith in the God who revealed himself in Jesus Christ. They used many different forms of thought and religious symbol to do this. Some proved adequate, some inadequate; and we shall have to examine the milieu of thought from which such terms as "Father," "Son," "Spirit," "begotten," "proceeding," and so on, are derived, and exactly what they meant, and may mean to us. What is imperative, however, to bear in mind in this connection, is that the New Testament betrays a marked development in the understanding of the revelation in Jesus Christ, and is not all of one piece so far as the symbols used are concerned. They differ considerably from one writer to another. One of the sources of the confusion in trinitarian theology is that the doctrine arose when this sense of the development of thought in the New Testament was lacking. Texts were torn from their contexts and misused to no small degree, and certain symbols were canonized without a full understanding of their original meaning. They were introduced into later theological schemes, not because they really fitted, but because they could not be questioned. Much of the defense of the Trinity as a "revealed" doctrine, is really an evasion of the objections that can be brought against it.

Certainly the New Testament writers were nearer the dramatic events by which God unveiled himself in Jesus Christ than we are, and surely the measure of their inspiration was greater than that of later theologians. Yet it is equally true that we profit from a benefit denied to them, viz., two thousand years of Christian reflection and experience. In consequence, while we must listen in humility to what they say, we must continue trying to express in ever clearer and more satisfactory ways the message they recorded. Indeed, the doctrine of the Trinity itself is part of that process. It is not a doctrine specifically to be found in the New Testament. It is a creation of the fourth-century Church. There are elements in the New Testament which point toward it, and others which point away from it, as we shall see later. But the important thing is this: The background of thought in Judaism and Hellenistic culture, whence the New Testament symbols for understanding Jesus Christ were drawn, was not necessarily the best. This background has bequeathed to theology innumerable problems; and the recent attempts to "demytheologize" the New Testament, while they may be unduly radical and unacceptable, do point to the constant need for us to weigh the value of New Testament symbolism and assess its adequacy. The modern study of the Bible both forbids us to deal with its text, out of its context, as many church fathers did, and also enriches our grasp of its message. We, then, like the New Testament writers, seek to express as adequately as possible the nature of this God who disclosed himself in Jesus Christ; and we should not feel bound by their particular symbolism if we find it at times detracts from, or confuses, the basic message it sought to convey.

This, of course, raises a fundamental issue which cannot be

fully discussed or solved here, viz., how can we distinguish the "basic message" from its symbolic clothing? Perhaps there is no ultimate answer to that dilemma, since the two are so inseparably tied together. Yet we can certainly make distinctions. It is one thing to call Jesus "Messiah," quite another to call him "Lord," and still another to call him "God." We may say, and rightly, he is all these things. Yet he transcends them all. The New Testament tells us something about God's revealing of himself which gives new meaning to all these terms, so that, for practical belief, they are identical. Yet this which lies behind them, is what we seek to express ever more adequately, and we may find some New Testament terms more helpful than others. We have a right, then, to exercise a critical judgment in our use of language to define the Christian faith; and we are not bound to the New Testament text in a slavish way, in dealing with such symbols as Father, Son, Spirit, and so on. Nor must we assume they always mean the same thing when we encounter them in the Scriptures. They mean different things, since there was a development in understanding and expressing the mystery of Jesus Christ. With these differences we shall have to deal, since they are pertinent to the formulation of the Trinity; and I shall try to show that many of the confusions in trinitarian doctrine derive from using ancient symbols to express ideas which they are not adequate to convey.

CHAPTER II

THE NATURE OF THE PROBLEM

IT IS GENERALLY ASSUMED THAT THE MAJOR PROBLEM IN TRINItarian doctrine concerns the way in which God can be one "person," yet three. This certainly is a real issue, but it is not the basic one. Others have felt that it is the place of the Spirit in the Trinity which is most difficult to explain and understand. This too is a significant question; yet it is secondary. Both these problems must be explored later in surveying the New Testament evidence and the classic patterns of trinitarian thinking. Here, however, I wish to point to what seems to me the most fundamental issue, and one which is often insufficiently examined, viz., the difference between the Father and the Son. All trinitarian theology ultimately hangs on this distinction, and it has been variously interpreted in Christian history. Why should we posit two terms, Father and Son, in the Godhead? In what way do they differ? It is often supposed that the answer to these questions is relatively simple. Theologians have generally contended that Father and Son differ in that the Son is derived from, or "begotten" from, the Father. But what does this really mean? In what sense can we say the one is begotten of the other?

The ideas of fatherhood and sonship in the Scriptures are examined in the next chapter. Here we are concerned only with a preliminary review of the issue. The basic distinction arose from the need to differentiate the humiliated and risen Jesus from the God of the Jewish tradition. Here was one person over against another person; and while the distinction was cast in many different forms—Jesus, for instance, was Messiah or Lord or Son of man, in contrast to God himself—the terms which finally prevailed to express the difference were those of Father and Son. They have their roots in the Old Testament, where they distinguish God from those of his creatures with whom he has a unique relation, who respond to his call, and who, recognizing their creaturely dependence upon him, yield themselves to the vocation he gives them. A crucial example is Ps. 2:7, where Israel's king, and perhaps the Messiah in later interpretation, is "this day" begotten of God. That is to say, he responds to God's call and is recognized as truly God's Son—something he was not fully until his vocation was both granted and accepted. Israel, similarly, as a people, is God's son, being created and chosen by him and fulfilling the destiny he appoints them (Deut. 32:6 ff.). This idea of the intimate relation between God as the heavenly Father and man as his son, was given new and richer meaning in the teaching of Jesus. God is the one whose all-embracing love includes all his children, both just and unjust, and whose nature man is called to imitate (Luke 6:35-6). Yet the deepest intimacy of this relation is reserved for Jesus himself. He, in a unique way, is God's Son, as chosen for a special vocation and doing God's will. At the baptism and transfiguration he is so marked (Mark 1:11; 9:7). Only he really knows the true nature of the Father (Luke 10:22). Yet this close relation, deep as it is, is far from a relation of equality or identity. Not even the Son knows the time of the End as the Father knows it (Mark 13:32).

Father and Son thus distinguish God and Jesus, in terms of

creation, adoption, and vocation. A further step is taken by Paul, for whom the term Son of God takes on a new meaning. The risen Jesus is God's Son by *nature,* while men are only sons of God by *adoption* (Gal. 4:4 ff.). He is a heavenly being "in the form of God" (Phil. 2:6), God's "image" and the "first-born of all creation" (Col. 1:15 R.S.V.). This transition from the relation of an earthly creature, the man Jesus of Nazareth, with his heavenly Father, to one of a relation between God and a supramundane being, represents the most fundamental step in the direction of trinitarian thinking. What does it involve?

It involves the idea that God works through his agents, which are angelic beings, but in the case of the Son more than that. He is higher than the angels; he is the image of God, through whom and for whom creation comes to be (Col. 1:16). Now this implies some sort of distinction within the Godhead itself. Paul never reaches an overt expression of this, but it is clear in John. Jesus is the Word, the Logos become incarnate (John 1:1). What does that mean? It means that the Word or Son is that aspect or "mode of being" of God whereby he comes into relationship with the world, whereby he creates and reveals himself.

Now this is a momentous idea. It rests on the assumption that God is absolutely transcendent, remote, invisible, unknowable and complete in himself, and yet related to the world, creating it and revealing himself. The distinction of Father and Son is thus a distinction about the paradoxical nature of God: absolutely above and beyond, and yet at the same time near and immanent. Such paradoxical statements we are forced to make on philosophical no less than on religious grounds. Philosophically we have somehow to apply to God the idea of the absolute—to say that he is alone, single, simple, incomparable, and so forth; for there cannot be two absolutes, since the one would qualify the other. Yet we have also to say that he comes into relationship. He creates; and by his doing so, the magic spell of his absolute nature is broken. The one is now involved in the many. The remoteness, the self-sufficiency, and the absolute transcendence of God, are overcome in his creating and being related to his creatures. The Christian doctrine of creation demands that we say these apparently contradictory things. He is absolute, yet he is also creator.

From a religious point of view, which is the more important from a Christian standpoint, we have to state a similar paradox. God is a jealous God; he brooks no rivals; he is the God of the prophetic tradition—the God whose glory is beyond our imagination, whose power is infinite, and whose demands are absolute. He has no consort like the gods of the nature religions, for this would compromise his unique glory and self-sufficiency. He stands in contrast to the manifoldness of his creatures, by the solemn character of his unity. He creates Eve as a helpmate for Adam, for he sees "it is not good that the man should be alone" (Gen. 2:18). But this marks the contrast between the creature and his God. Man exists in society; God exists alone.

Yet God is related to his creatures, and this requires that his absolute transcendence be set over against his love and creativity. This is expressed in varied ways in the Scriptures, and there is some ambiguity in the symbols for it, since the Hebrew writers in general were not concerned with the philosophic problem of the absolute coming into relation, which we have treated above. Sometimes (and especially in moments of great crisis) God acts directly, as a great king will lead his armies personally in battle. Sometimes he acts by means of his "Spirit" or "wisdom" or "name," sometimes by his "angel" or "messenger" (as a great king will function through intermediaries). It is not necessary to trace the Old Testament development in this connection. It is complex and difficult. The central point to observe, however, is that the more God's transcendent glory is stressed, the more need there is for intermediaries. Especially is this to be seen in the intertestamental literature, where God's wisdom and heavenly beings, like the "Son of man" in Enoch, are introduced to guard God's glory and yet establish his relation with the world.

Now, it is from this background of the need for intermediaries that the relation of Father to Son in terms of heavenly realities, in contrast to the earlier distinction between the heavenly Father and his creatures, arose. The Son of God in Paul and the Logos or Word in John are expressions of the belief that God is both absolutely transcendent and yet related to his creatures. He creates and reveals not directly, but by his Son or Logos. The Father thus stands for God in his beyondness, the Son for God in his relatedness. In Paul, to be sure, the problem is not so simple as that, for he never calls the Son of God or Lord (*Kyrios*) specifically "God." That occurs first in John (1:1) and in the Epistles to Titus (2:13). Yet behind the whole development there lies this basic factor: Father and Son are distinguished in order to guard the absolute character and transcendent glory of God on the one hand, and to affirm on the other that the created world is *his,* and not an emanation from him or the result of some decline in the heavenly sphere or the work of an inferior God (as in Gnosticism). God is *beyond* and yet he is *related;* that is the essence of the distinction between Father and Son.

It was not, indeed, until considerably later than the New Testament that the full implications of this were seen, and a more adequate way of expressing it in the eternal generation of the

Son was elaborated. Of this I shall speak later. My concern here is to point out that the terms Father and Son underwent a radical transformation in the New Testament. Whereas they originally referred to a relation between God and his chosen, earthly servant, they came to denote a relationship in the heavenly sphere, which was determined by the principle of mediation. The Son was God in action—creating, revealing, incarnate, and sitting now at his Father's right hand. The Father was God in his absolute and transcendent glory.

But that is not the whole story, for a remarkable confusion enters in, due to the nature of the symbolism itself. While the term Father came to denote God in his absolute character, it could never be divested of its original content. It referred to the heavenly Father who was related to his children and who created, disciplined, loved, redeemed, and judged them. Thus an ambiguity of no small proportions enters into the use of the term. While on the one hand it symbolized God's remote and absolute transcendence, on the other it stood (as it had stood in the Hebrew tradition and in the teaching of Jesus) for God in his relationship to his people. This ambiguity has beset trinitarian thinking down the ages, and the attempts to solve the problem will be examined later. Here I only point out that it is a fundamental issue in the use of the term.

The basic problem of trinitarian thinking is to establish what precisely we mean by contrasting the Father and the Son. I have tried to show that, as far as these terms are used in reference to the Godhead, they distinguish God as absolute and transcendent from God as active and related to his world. That is what lies behind their use in John and Paul, though it is to be admitted that these authors are far from consistent in following this pattern through. This is due to many factors, such as the ambiguity of the term Father, and the reluctance of Paul to regard the Son as fully God. He views him as a heavenly being in the "form" of God, with only a temporary authority which he finally yields to the Father (I Cor. 15:28). Yet it is the underlying problem, rather than its precise New Testament expression, with which we are here concerned. The Father is God in his beyondness; the Son is God in his action and revelation.

Now the question to be asked is whether these symbols are adequate to convey this meaning. And here our first objection to trinitarian doctrine must be entered. Not only is the term Father highly ambiguous, as we have seen, but also it is doubtful that there is value in thinking of these two paradoxical aspects or "modes of being" [1] in God under terms which imply the one is derived from the other. Is there any real significance in saying that God in his action and revelation is begotten of God in his transcendent glory? Why must we assume the one is prior to the other, in any sense? Ought we not rather to say that here we have one of many antinomies which reach to the confines of human reason? We shall discuss others later, such as God's wrath over against his love, his joy over against his participation in man's suffering for man's redemption, his being the ground of our existence and yet the object of our dialogue with him. There are many distinctions to be made in reference to the Godhead,

[1] Throughout this book I have retained this phrase "mode of being" to refer to God in his absolute character as well as to God as revealed, related, and encountered. Properly speaking, however, I should really refer to the former as a mode of nonbeing, since God, in this respect being "above being," can only be fittingly denominated by terms of the negative theology. As absolute, God is not being, but transcends being. He is the abyss, the void, and so forth. Only by such expressions can one denote that positive aspect of God whereby he transcends all that is relative.

in order that we may preserve the full truth of the Christian faith. But this basic paradox of God Beyond and God Related is one of them, and the terms Father and Son do not illuminate it. Rather they becloud it. They suggest the priority of his transcendence, which is an unwarranted assumption, and they introduce much ambiguity into the issue we are trying to clarify. For instance, the Father is often thought of as the Creator. But he cannot possibly be that, if we reserve the term Son for God in his activity. Or if we say that both Father and Son are equally creator, or even that the Father is creator through the Son, we have destroyed our fundamental distinction, viz., that when we say "Father" we mean God in his beyondness, and when we say "Son" we mean God creating and revealing. The fact is that the terms are highly ambiguous and confusing, and the subtlety which is often found in trinitarian writers really derives from the use of inadequate terms and symbols. But if we appreciate how these terms arose, and if we penetrate to the real problems underlying them, we may save ourselves much unnecessary labor and confusion. If we realize that terms which once defined a relation between God and his creatures, were later transposed to the heavenly sphere to express a principle of mediation within the context of intermediaries, and if we appreciate that the issue which underlay this transposition was inaedquately expressed by these terms, we shall not need to pose for ourselves the kind of subtle and sophisticated questions which often characterize trinitarian writing. Into some of these we shall later enter. What is to be stressed here is that the terms Father and Son are inadequate to define the fundamental distinction of God in his beyondness and God in his relatedness. The one is not derived from the other. They are paradoxical modes of God's being, of which we can say no more than that we believe he is one, transcendent in glory and beyond all thought and comprehension, self-sufficient and alone; and yet we equally affirm he is the creator of the world, related to his children and revealing himself to them above all in the mighty act of Jesus Christ.

A last point may be made. One of the reasons why the particular terms Father and Son were transposed to the heavenly sphere was that God should be distinguished from the risen Jesus. But this distinction was overcome in later Christian thinking. It did not suffice to say that the risen Jesus was some created, heavenly being, as he is in Paul (Col. 1:15). He was God made flesh. In him God himself was taking action in human history, revealing himself and recreating his fallen world. In consequence God in Christ could not be Son, as inferior to God. It was the humanity, the human Jesus, which was inferior to God. But once this was established (and the point will be pursued further in later chapters), why should God in Christ continue to be called Son? It is God as related to his world, revealing and redeeming, who is present. And while this must be distinguished from God in his absolute transcendence, the terms Father and Son are inadequate to express this, as I have tried to show.

CHAPTER III

THE NEW TESTAMENT MATRIX

THE NEW TESTAMENT PRESENTS US WITH THREE DOMINANT SYMbols of the Godhead—Father, Son, and Spirit; and it is from this fact that trinitarian theology has arisen. The Scriptures, to be sure, use many other terms in reference to God; but they can all, in one way or another, be reduced to these three. That does not mean that a certain overlapping and ambiguity are not involved in the process of so reducing them. This will become apparent as we proceed with our study. But it does mean that a threefold distinction is reasonably clear in the New Testament, and the formulas of Matt. 28:19 and II Cor. 13:14 bear witness to this. These formulas themselves may be somewhat removed from the subsequent trinitarian doctrines in intention, and may imply ideas which were later abandoned; but they do point to the fact that early Christian thinking and experience centered itself in three dominant ways of considering God and his operations. It will be my purpose now to analyze the meaning of these three symbols as we encounter them and their synonyms in the Bible, and to deal more fully with the issues touched on in the preceding chapter.

THE FATHER

God is first of all "Father." As such he has a special relation to Israel. In the wilderness he "carried" them, as a man is wont to carry his son (Deut. 1:31). He chastens them as a father disciplines his family (Deut. 8:5), loves and pities them as a father cares for his children (Hos. 11:1; Ps. 103:13). This authority and love he exercises are due to his being their creator (Deut. 32:6 ff.; Isa. 64:8), and especially rest upon the fact that he has chosen Israel to be his special people and to assign them a unique vocation (Deut. 32:6 ff.). The Old Testament fatherhood of God is not a general fatherhood dependent only upon his creating Israel. It involves a special relationship, due to his election of them as a chosen people. Hence, when the relation is considered in terms of a particular person, such as Israel's king in Ps. 2:7, the theme of adoption enters in. "Thou art my Son; this day have I begotten thee," refers to the fact that the king is not really a son by having been created, but becomes a son in a full sense by being chosen and adopted to fulfill a unique role for God. *"This day* have I begotten thee"—chosen you to be something that formerly you were not.

In the teaching of Jesus this paternal relation of God to man is given new and deeper meaning. No term is more basic to his message. The Father's love and care, his intimate concern for the smallest details of the life of his creatures, his demands, his glory, and his yearning for his children, are fundamental to Jesus' message. Nor does the Father's love know artificial limits. It is all-embracing. It does not stop with his chosen people or with the "just" who respond to his call. It includes even the unjust, and the disciple is bidden to imitate this character of the Father (Luke 6:35-6).

The primary ideas, then, of fatherhood as applied to God are those of creation and vocation. These themes will become of importance when we examine later the concept of sonship, and its special application to Jesus. Here we must now consider the more general significance of the symbol Father, in connection with both God's transcendence and his relation to the world.

Because he is creator, God is *above* his creation. Thus the term implies something of God's holy glory and his mystery, as well as his intimacy with his creation. To a child fatherhood means two things. It means a relation of love and care and discipline, but it means also a relation of mystery. The father is the one who is above restraint. He comes and goes as he pleases. He has a unique power that can terrify the child as well as awaken his admiration. He is in some way mysterious in his strength and stature and knowledge. Hence the symbol as applied to God refers both to transcendence and to relationship. It hints at the fact that God is beyond as well as near, that he is wholly other as well as the One who loves and pities.

The early art form by which his was given expression in Christianity is that of a hand being stretched forth from a cloud of light. Out of the mystery of the divine glory God appears to take action in human history. This iconography may perhaps go back to the cult of Sabazius, but it appears early in Christianity, a notable example being that of the sarcophagus of Junius Bassus in the fourth century. It is found too in later Judaism, where, for instance, the hand of God is shown arresting Abraham from sacrificing Isaac, in the third-century fresco at Dura-Europos.

This symbolism of the hand of God derives from many Old Testament passages (Ps. 10:12; 31:5; 80:17; Isa. 41:20; etc.), and is a metaphor for God in action. Emerging from the mystery of his glory, by his hand or his right arm he does things. Artistic expressions of God the Father in the form of a human person are very rare up to the tenth century. Before that period the Father was depicted as both transcendent and related, by means of this hand reaching down from the cloud of glory. But this symbol came to involve an ambiguity both in Christian art and in Christian theology. For when an attempt was made to guard God's transcendence by introducing intermediates (such as his Word or wisdom or angel) as the means of God's action, they were really duplication of the hand stretched forth from heaven. God was doing things by his right hand, and yet at the same time he was doing the *same* things by his Word or Spirit. This ambiguity is to be seen very clearly in Philo, whose union of Jewish with Greek thinking is characteristic of a good deal of New Testament symbolism. Whether derived from Philo or not, it is reflected in Col. 1:15 ff., John's prologue, and Heb. 1-2.

Philo inherited from the Hebrew tradition the conviction of a God who is active, who intervenes directly in human history, and who, while sometimes employing intermediaries, does not stand in need of them. He is the direct source of the principal boons which man enjoys, as, for instance, the initial health of the body. Similarly he directly caused the plagues by which Israel finally gained freedom from Egypt (*Leg. All.* 3.177; *Vit. Mos.* 1.17 .97; 23.130). As such God is the Father of all and the Creator (*De Fug.* 13.29; *De Opific* 24).

But Philo introduces a second theme derived from Greek thinking, viz., that God creates by his Word or Logos. This theme has a dual root. On the one hand it stems from a view of God as the abstract God, the Absolute, who does not have an immediate relation with the world, but who necessarily operates through intermediaries. These intermediaries are derived from an analysis of abstract thought and mind. God is the thinker, and he operates in terms of his reason by projecting his thoughts. These thoughts are the mediating principles between him and the world. Of these principles the primary or dominant one is the Word or Logos.

A second root of the idea is closely related to this, viz., that God creates in much the same way as a man creates. First he conceives an idea, then he executes it. First he formed the intelligible world, and then on the basis of this pattern he made the sensible world, just as we first conceive our idea and then work it out in material terms. For Philo this universe of ideas exists *in* the divine reason (*De Opific.* 16 ff.); and the divine reason is thus the *instrument of creation* through which the universe is formed (*De Cherub.* 35.127; *Sac. Abel et Cain* 8-9). The distinction between the divine reason itself and the Logos or Word as the expression of this is not altogether clear in Philo. The difficulty goes back to the fact that Logos means both these things, but it is not necessary to pursue that question here. It suffices to stress that by an analysis of thought Philo reaches the conclusion that the intermediary principle of the Logos is the means by which God acts. Now the implication of this would be that God *always* acts that way. How could he create or do anything without his reason or the ideas he has? But this is not so in Philo. He never fully integrates his conception of God's *direct* action with his idea that God operates by his Logos.

Moreover, the Hebraic inheritance of God's direct intervention does not fit a third theme which enters into Philo's thought, viz., that God requires intermediaries, since he cannot come into contact with matter and is himself not the immediate source of evil. Since God's nature, says Philo, is blessed, it forbids that he should touch "the limitless and chaotic matter" (*De Spec. Leg.* 1.328-9). Instead, he made use of the incorporeal powers, the thoughts or ideas he had, which are distinguished from him.

What Philo calls "the secondary boons"—the health, for instance, which is enjoyed *after* sickness—involve evil as their presupposition. These are granted not directly by God, but by his angels or Logoi (Thoughts: *Leg. All.* 3.178). So in the creation of man, while God directly made his "sovereign part" (his mind and consciousness), the powers whom he addressed when he said, "Let *us* make man"; these he employed to create the "subject" part of man and the evil things that affect his soul. "It could not be that the Father could be the cause of an evil thing to his offspring; and vice and vicious activities are an evil thing" (*De Opific.* 75; *De Fug.* 68 ff.).

From these observations it becomes clear that there is an essential ambiguity in Philo's thought, an ambiguity which we shall find running through trinitarian thinking. On the one hand God acts *directly,* and on the other *indirectly*. In the one case the Father is the God of the Hebrew tradition who emerges from his glory to take immediate action; on the other hand the Father is the abstract and absolute God who operates through the Logos and sundry other powers. These have their roots in an analysis of abstract thought and in the need to separate God from contact with what is material and evil. In the Christian tradition this latter consideration is not important, since the material creation is viewed as originally good, not as bordering on evil, as in Philo. The general problem of evil, moreover, does not enter into our consideration, since the duality of good and evil in Christianity is not connected with the need for God to have intermediaries. Evil has its origin in the Fall, and does not touch the issue of God's creativity. But the point of importance concerns the ambiguity about God's direct and indirect action. There is a fundamental discrepancy between a view of the Father as he appears in Hebrew thought, and a view of the Father as the abstract God who operates by his reason or Logos. On the one hand it is the Father who is the Creator; on the other hand the term Father is reserved for God in his absolute transcendence, while it is his Word or Logos which is the means of creation. In iconography we can say that the hand of God emerging from the cloud of glory represents God's *direct* action; but this same activity of God is *duplicated* by the ideas of the Spirit and the Word, which do precisely the same things and which are portrayed in scenes of the baptism of Jesus, for instance, by the dove and by Jesus himself.

One final point may be mentioned in this connection. The idea that the Logos is begotten by God, is his "first-born," his "invisible image," and so on, plays an important role in Philo, and whether directly from him or not, comes into Christian thinking (*De Conf. Ling.* 146 ff.). It derives from an analysis of abstract thought. The mind begets the idea, and as we have seen, the idea or Word is for Philo the intermediary between God and his action. Now the serious question arises whether this is an adequate way of describing the difference between God as absolutely transcendent and as related to his world. There are several objections to be made to the symbolism. For one thing, an analysis of human thought can never provide the real distinction we are trying to make. For this distinction is paradoxical in a way human thinking is not. The thinker does not stand in relation to his thought in the same way that God's absolute character contrasts with his being related to the world. While the thinker transcends his thought, he is its originator. But this is precisely *not* what we are trying to say of God. His transcendence is absolute: it is not a transcendence of origination. He is beyond, but he is also related; and the beyondness is not in any sense prior to the relatedness, nor does it engender it. If it did engender it, it would no longer be the kind of absolute beyondness of which we are speaking. The weakness of this analogy with God is the weakness of all such analogies which try to speak of God's absolute character in relative terms, and to compose a paradox by introducing a false kind of unity and simplicity. If we imagine that God creates in a way not dissimilar from the way man creates (and such analogies are useful and necessary), we speak only of that aspect of God whereby he is *related* to us. We say nothing of his absolute glory and the way he is beyond, remote, and totally inaccessible. By analyzing human thought or any human activity we can gain some hint of how God is *near* us, who are made in his image, but of his absolute transcendence and beyondness we can say nothing. Here we reach the void of his glory, the "nothingness" of his being, the abyss of his power. We can speak only in negations; and no relative terms can even hint at what we are trying to say. It is for that reason that the idea of the Father begetting the Son or Word is so misleading, insofar as what is being described by these terms is God's absolute character over against his self-revealing and creative activity. We have reached the limits of human thought and analogy; and we can say no more than that he is absolutely beyond and yet related. Here is a final paradox; and no analysis of thought or creative activity is going to help us to compose it. Rather will such analyses *confuse* it, for, taken as they are from relative creatures, they will miss the essential point which is the *absolute* character of God's transcendence.

Another reason why this analogy of "begetting" is misleading lies in the fact that it assumes the priority of God's beyondness.

But we have no reason to suppose this. He is these two things; he exists in these two modes of being—but neither is prior to the other. In no sense can we say he is *first* the all-glorious, and *then* able to be related to his creation. His capacity for action is not secondary to his absolute character. In one of the most thorough and serious attempts recently to deal with the Trinity, Karl Barth posits the difference between Father and Son in terms of God's revelation. I shall have more to say of his treatment in a later chapter. Here I would only note his major distinction: that in revelation God distinguishes himself from himself. It is his property "hiddenly to be God and yet at the same time and in quite another way, namely, manifestly, i.e. in the form of something He Himself is not, to be God a second time."[1] The distinction between Father and Son is that between God as veiled and God as unveiled. This is a way of putting the basic distinction we have made between God in his beyondness and God in his relatedness. But Barth makes the second dependent upon the first. And why? Because he assumes that God by his nature *"cannot be unveiled to man,"*[2] and hence in revelation has to become "God a second time." But this assumption is unwarranted. We have no reason for claiming that God by his nature is such that, *first,* he cannot be unveiled to man, and so has to make himself God a *second* time, as if the first mode of his being were the prior one. All we are justified in saying is that God by his nature exists in these two modes, unveiled and veiled, related and beyond. But that the one is prior to the other in any sense cannot be assumed. All we can assume is that as absolutely beyond, God

[1] *The Doctrine of the Word of God,* tr. G. T. Thomson (New York: Charles Scribner's Sons, 1936, 1949), Vol. I, Pt. 1, p. 363.

[2] *Ibid.,* p. 362.

cannot be unveiled to man, but that as related, he *can*. It is his character to be both; and he is not more God or "first" God one way or the other. The implication of saying the Father begets the Son, is that of assuming God's glory and self-sufficiency are antecedent to his capacity to be in relationship, and in some sense *cause* it. But this goes back to using false analogies when trying to express the paradoxical nature of God's being.

A further objection to describing the distinction between God's beyondness and his relatedness in terms derived from abstract thought, concerns the validity of finding the image of God in man's ability to think. I shall have more to say of this later. It will suffice here merely to raise the question whether intellectual categories, which are abstractions from man's total being, are a particularly helpful way of thinking about God. But in any case, so far as we use them, they are altogether insufficient to denote the essential paradox of his beyondness and his relatedness. The only way in which they might prove useful is in saying something about how he is *related* to us.

It is, however, not only the defect of the intellectual analogy which is open to criticism in the notion that God's absolute character begets his relatedness. Behind the analogy itself lies one of the most pregnant ideas which has influenced Christian theology, but one which is involved in a logical inconsistency. It is the concept of the fecundity of the Absolute, which was clearly enunciated in Plotinus, but foreshadowed by Plato. In order to relate the Absolute to the world, it was assumed that the Absolute, considered as the "idea of the good," was "overflowing" in its nature, and moved itself to creation by its own superabundance. We are not concerned here with the way this supposition can or cannot be related to the Christian conception of creation out of nothing, but rather with its consequences for the Logos doctrine and the understanding of the Godhead. In this connection the assumption is that the Word is begotten of the Father, because the Father as absolute overflows in his goodness and projects his "idea"—the Word. The inconsistency in this notion is twofold: on the one hand the idea of "overflowing" compromises the absolute character of the Father. If there is something "over," this implies a defect in the self-sufficient and simple essence of God. There is a "remainder" outside the boundary—the "limitless" boundary, to be sure—of the Absolute. On the other hand, the begotten image is inferior to the Father,[3] and this in Plotinus is the explanation of the graded hierarchy of being with its ladder of increasing defect. But it is never explained how the Absolute could generate what is inferior to itself. Indeed, there is a logical inconsistency in the idea. It is impossible to bring the notions of absoluteness and relatedness into any kind of relation, precisely because the terms themselves preclude this. All it is possible to say is that both these principles exist in God, and neither is prior to the other. It is a final paradox. But every attempt to compose it only introduces confusion and inconsistency. The paradox can never be overcome, and the very attempt to do so can only prove artificial.

THE SON

The essential ambiguity of the term Father, standing at once for the Hebrew God who acts directly in history (though sometimes employing intermediaries as a great king might), and also

[3] Of the inequality of the Son to the Father as *persons* of the Trinity more will be said later. However much their equality may be stressed in their sharing the divine essence, their inequality becomes apparent in that the Son, and not the Father, is the agent of creation and is incarnate.

for his absolute transcendence in contrast to his creative and revealing activity, must now engage our attention in its relation to the Son.

First and foremost in the New Testament the sonship of Jesus means the dependence of the man, Jesus of Nazareth, upon his heavenly Father. The Father is the "Lord of heaven and earth" (Luke 10:21), whom Jesus addresses in the garden of Gethsemane by the intimate and intensive word, "Abba" (Mark 14:36), and who acknowledges Jesus as his Son at the baptism and the transfiguration (Mark 1:11; 9:7). The application of Ps. 2:7 to Jesus is in intent probably messianic, though there is no sure evidence that this psalm was so understood in Judaism. In any case the term came to denote that in a special way Jesus was God's Son, as having been given the vocation of the Messiah and having fulfilled it in God's purpose (cf. Mark 1:11; Acts 13:33; Heb. 1:5).

There is no uniform conception in the New Testament concerning the moment when Jesus became the Messiah. Rather does the New Testament betray a development in this regard. It may be that the earliest Christian preaching is reflected in Acts 2–5, and that the most primitive idea was that Jesus became Son in this special sense, and hence Lord and Saviour, at his resurrection (2:36; 5:31; 13:33). A vestige of this notion perhaps survives in Rom. 1:4, where Jesus is designated Son of God in power by his resurrection from the dead. It became clear, however, that if Jesus was Messiah *then,* he must have been so before. It seemed right, therefore, to assume that at the very beginning of his ministry—at his baptism, in fact—his vocation had been given to him, and he in turn had responded to it.[4] But even this failed

[4] The transfiguration story may be a reading back into the ministry of the resurrection appearances.

to suffice. If Jesus was already Messiah at his baptism, he must have been such by his birth. Hence the story of the Nativity, and indeed of the Conception. Only one who had been born of the Spirit could really fulfill this destiny.

Yet even that could not entirely account for the mighty acts God had done in Jesus. Not by God's creation of a special human being through his dynamic power or Spirit, could the Saviour arise. Rather must the Saviour be one who descended from the heavenly sphere. He was not merely a creature born of Mary and Spirit, but a heavenly being who was clothed with flesh. Thus we arrive at the unique element in Paul's view: the incarnation of a pre-existent being. This is the point of the hymn in Phil. 2:6 ff. and of the account in Col. 1:15 ff. (cf. II Cor. 8:9). In the former, Christ is "in the form of God," a heavenly being who, unlike Satan, does not grasp at equality with God, but is content to accept a humiliating vocation. In consequence God elevates him to the unique place of "Lord." Colossians goes further than this and hints at the Logos Christology. Christ is the agent of creation and the image of God. The climax comes with the prologue of John. There the elements of subordination to be found in Paul, are finally done away with. The Son is no longer merely the *Kyrios,* with a temporary authority to be surrendered ultimately to the Father (I Cor. 15:28), and himself only "in the form of God." Now in John he becomes "God," the Logos from all eternity (John 1:1).

Whether this development is strictly chronological or not, it is not possible to say. It may be that these diverse ideas existed side by side in different geographical localities. However that may be, what is important to notice is the way in which the term Son becomes transposed to the heavenly sphere. It refers not to the relation of the human Jesus to his heavenly Father, but to a relation within the Godhead. The idea that Jesus was "adopted" by God, which lies behind the use of Ps. 2:7—"*this day* have I begotten thee" (i.e., to be Son in a unique way, which you were not before), is abandoned. Jesus is God's "*own* Son," in contrast to men who can become sons only by adoption (Gal. 4:3 ff.; Rom. 8:3, 23). In John's writing there is even an attempt to reserve the word Son (*huios*) exclusively for Christ. Men are "children" (*tekna*) by contrast.

There are other terms applied to Christ in the New Testament. The heavenly figure of the Son of man, for instance, derived from Daniel and Enoch, plays no small role. But it is not necessary here to survey them all, since they do not have a bearing on the trinitarian issue. So far as they are heavenly intermediaries, as is the Son of man, the subordinationist element is overcome with the Johannine application of "God" and "Logos" to Jesus.

What occurred, then, in the development was the granting of a truly divine status to Jesus the Christ. It was God himself who was at work in Jesus of Nazareth. As pre-existent he was creator and God's Word, the means by which God comes into relation and is active. "All things were made by him; and without him was not any thing made that was made" (John 1:3). The distinction, then, of Father and Son is one which contrasts God's absolute transcendence with his creative and revealing activity. "No one has ever seen God; the only Son, who is in the bosom of the Father, he has made him known" (John 1:18). Because, however, the term Father had a very different connotation in the Jewish tradition and in the teaching of Jesus, it was seldom strictly used in this sense in the New Testament. While some passages indicate that Father and Son refer exclusively to the relations in the Godhead or in the heavenly sphere, others are determined by the more primitive tradition by which we say "Our Father." Trinitarian theology, as we shall see in a later chapter, has tried to solve this discrepancy by a subtle doctrine of "appropriations" and by regarding the whole Trinity, and not the Father only, as referred to in the address of the Lord's Prayer. But this kind of subtlety is surely an unnecessary exercise for the intellect. The real problem goes back to the fact that the terms Father and Son are really inadequate to describe the kind of distinction we are trying to make in the Godhead. If by Son we mean God in his active relations with us—creating, redeeming, and revealing—then it would be far simpler and clearer to call this "God-in-Action," "God Related," God in his mode of being as revealer and creator, than to say "Son." For this latter term involves all the difficulties we have already examined in connection with the idea of begetting.

The reason why this symbolism was riveted on the Church is twofold. In the earlier stages of Christian reflection a sharp distinction between God and his servant was made. In general, Jewish monotheism forbade thinking of the Messiah (the first title by which Jesus was understood) as much more than a human being. He was Son in a special sense, but only as a human being with a unique endowment of Spirit and a unique vocation. As Christian reflection proceeded and the inadequacy of such a view became apparent, the term was reinterpreted to mean a heavenly being (the Primal Man, perhaps), and finally to refer to a distinction in the Godhead itself. But this reinterpretation really necessitated abandoning the original term, if the full implications of the divine reality of Jesus Christ were to be expressed. Yet the traditional terminology stood in the way of such a radical change, and the term has remained to plague trinitarian thinking.

The other reasons for the retention of the terms were the Greek background of the Logos doctrine, and the attempt to understand God's activity in terms derived from the analysis of abstract thought. The Word is begotten of the Mind. But this, as we have seen, is a false attempt to compose the fundamental paradox of God's being as both beyond and related. An analysis of thought can never provide a fitting analogy to this; and there is no way by which the absolute transcendence of God and his relatedness can be brought into a coherent unity. All we can say is that God is *both,* and leave it at that. As soon as we try to find a way by which God transcends and overcomes this and other antinomies which we are forced to hold, we destroy the very nature of the antinomies, and sacrifice one or the other horn of the dilemma. Either we remove God so far from the world that he can never be related to it, or we relate him so closely to it that we sacrifice his transcendence.

In short, the terms Father and Son are inadequate symbols to describe the nature of God's being; and by retaining them we introduce a confusion into our thinking and pose for ourselves a variety of unnecessary and insoluble problems which stem directly from the unfitting nature of our original terms. Son is fitting, to be sure, when applied to the humanity of Christ. When we think of Jesus of Nazareth in his relation to his heavenly Father, we understand what sonship means. But this is very different from trying to apply the same category to a distinction in the Godhead. Whatever way we state the Christological issue and try to relate the divine and the human in Jesus Christ, we must avoid applying to the divine what is appropriate merely to the human. Because we can say no less than that it was God himself who was involved in the mighty acts of Jesus Christ, revealing himself and accomplishing the world's salvation, we shall find the title Son inappropriate for this. A distinction in the Godhead certainly we have to make. He who is absolutely transcendent is at the same time the one who is related to us and unveiled in Jesus. To fail to make the distinction is to compromise the divine transcendence. Yet the distinction cannot be adequately made by the terms Father and Son. They derive originally from a relation of God to the creature and never can be sufficiently divested of their origin to illuminate or to express a distinction within the Godhead itself.

THE SPIRIT

The place of the Spirit in the Trinity has long been regarded as one of the difficult aspects of that doctrine. Not until Augustine was there a thorough attempt to find a fitting reason for the existence of the Spirit as the third term of the Godhead, and to ground it ontologically in the divine life. Long before him, to be sure, the Trinity had been affirmed, and the solution of the problem at which he arrived had been foreshadowed by earlier thinkers. But it is first in Augustine that the distinctive nature of the Spirit and his place in the Trinity is given classic expression. Of this I shall speak in a later chapter. Here we shall be concerned with the biblical doctrine, and we shall see that the wide range of meaning given to "Spirit" is such that to distinguish it (or him) from Father and Son is at times difficult and even impossible. It is, indeed, the ambiguity of the term in the Scriptures which is responsible for the fact that a satisfactory doctrine of the Spirit was so long in developing; and some kind of adequate solution was only finally reached by means of arbitrary distinctions which could not fully cover the biblical material. The term Spirit became limited in meaning to only some of the ideas associated with it in the Scriptures.

The primary notion of Spirit in the Bible is that of God's dynamic activity. The Spirit is his breath, hence his vitality or life. Since a body without breath is dead, breath was viewed as the vitalizing element in man. At man's creation God breathed into Adam's nostrils the breath of life, and thus he became a living soul (Gen. 2:7). As applied to God, then, his breath is his vitality and the means by which he does things and expresses his creative potency.

From this fundamental conception some three central themes developed around the symbolism of God's Spirit.

First the Spirit is *creative*. It breathes over the chaos of the waters in Gen. 1:2 and appears to be the vital power by which God's command or "word" is fulfilled. It is like his fingers, whereby he frames the heavens, in Ps. 8:3; and indeed the finger of God in Luke 11:20 becomes the Spirit of God in the parallel passage of Matt. 12:28. The hand of God, his wisdom, Word, glory, and name, are all synonyms or variants of this basic idea of God's creative and ruling power. In the creation of Jesus it is the Spirit which forms the child in the womb of Mary (Matt. 1:20; Luke 1:35), and it is the Spirit which creates the Church and conceives the new life in the Christian (Gal. 5:22 ff.).

But the Spirit is also the power of *ecstasy*—the means whereby man is raised by God to a new level. When the Spirit falls upon him he is enabled to prophesy (often in Ezekiel; Joel 2:28 ff.;

John 16:13). The distinction between Spirit and Word in this connection is not a fundamental one. The great Old Testament prophets (e.g., Jeremiah, First and Second Isaiah) had avoided the term Spirit when referring to their inspiration, and preferred the term Word, in order to distinguish their work from the formless and ecstatic utterances of the reckless Nebiim. But Spirit and Word meant the same thing, viz., God's immanent presence whereby man's natural capacities were transcended. So it is that the Spirit is the internal witness by which a Christian is enabled to confess his Lord before his persecutors (Matt. 10:20; Mark 13:11; Luke 12:12), to recognize his adoption by God as a son (Rom. 8:16), and to call Christ "Lord" (I Cor. 12:3). Again, the Spirit is the Paraclete or Counselor, who leads the disciple into all truth, recalls the words of Jesus, and glorifies Christ (John 16:13-14; 14:26). The Spirit intercedes for us in prayer (Rom. 8:26) and is the means by which God adopts his creatures to be his sons (Ps. 2:7; of Jesus at his baptism, Mark 1:11; of Christians, Gal. 4:5-6).

Finally, the Spirit is connected with *the end of history*. A distinctive mark of God's Kingdom is the outpouring of the Spirit at the end of days, when prophecy, dream, and vision will characterize all ages and both sexes, and signs and wonders will appear on earth and in heaven in the great and terrible day of the Lord (Joel 2:28 ff.).

The wide use of the term "Spirit" in early Christianity is due to the ecstatic experience of the primitive church. The text of Joel cited above is used in Peter's first sermon at Pentecost to explain the utterances of the apostles. The day of the Lord had already arrived with the triumph of the Messiah in his resurrection (Acts 2:17 ff., 33 ff.), and with the consequent sending of the Spirit (Acts 2:32).

The Spirit thus is a term of wide meaning. It covers all of God's dynamic action and is closely related to, and even synonymous with, many other expressions. However, the New Testament distinguishes the Spirit from Christ, and it is important to understand the ways in which the difference is conceived.

In the early attempts to "explain" Jesus, the Spirit is the vitality of God whereby Jesus is raised from the dead (Rom. 1:4, the "spirit of holiness" is the Holy Spirit). Then again, the Spirit is seen as the divine power by which he is adopted for the messianic mission at his baptism (Mark 1:11), and the creative energy by which he is conceived in the womb (Matt. 1:20). These appear to be attempts to press ever further back, to his very conception, that union of God with man upon which the Messiah's vocation rested. In such explanations it is clear that Spirit and Jesus are always distinguished. The one is God's dynamic vitality and power; the other is the man Jesus who is endowed with Spirit to fulfill his special mission. But when it became apparent that such explanations were unsatisfactory—that salvation could only be understood in deeper terms, and that Jesus was not merely a "spirit" man—the problem of contrasting Jesus and the Spirit became more difficult. For the attempt to press still further back the divine reality in Jesus and to see him first as a heavenly being descending from the celestial sphere (Phil. 2:6 ff.), and then finally as the very image of God himself and the agent of creation (Col. 1:15 ff.; Heb. 1:2-3), made it difficult to say in what way he differed from the Spirit. For he fulfilled precisely the function of the Logos (John 1:1), which was the same as that of God's vital breath or power or word. Jesus was not merely a creation of Mary and Spirit, but the incarnate Word himself.

Yet the distinction is retained throughout the New Testament, though the logic would have been finally to identify them. If God himself was at work in Jesus of Nazareth, if he was the incarnation of God, then no distinction between the divine in Jesus and God's Spirit is really cogent. The contrast only held good as long as one was distinguishing the Spirit-endowed or Spirit-created man, and the Spirit itself. For God's vital potency or breath, is not something distinguishable from his Word or image. They are metaphorical ways of talking about the same thing—God in his relations with the world. The distinction henceforth should have been only between the humanity and the divinity, between the God who was present in Jesus, and the man or flesh in terms of which he was present. A distinction between two kinds of God-in-Relation, one called "Word" and the other "Spirit," was really untenable. There was no more point in contrasting them than in contrasting God's hand and his fingers.

This is the source of some difficulty in Paul's theology, and it will bear further examination. Spirit, in Paul, is the vital, dynamic energy of God, which is peculiarly evident in the signs and wonders accompanying his mission (Rom. 15:19). It is by the Spirit that his preaching is made effectual (I Cor. 2:4), and the many gifts displayed by his converts—gifts of faith, wisdom, tongues, miracles, healings, and so on—are acquired and exercised. But it is especially as the source of right teaching and revelation that the Spirit interests Paul (I Cor. 2:13; Eph. 3:5). From the Spirit derives the internal witness by which a man can recognize Jesus as Lord (I Cor. 12:3). Not, that is, by himself—

by a man's own natural reason or inclination—can the revelation of God in Christ be either acknowledged or appropriated. This is the work rather of the Spirit, who both intercedes for us (Rom. 8:26 ff.), and witnesses "with our spirit, that we are the children of God" (Rom. 8:16). To put it briefly, the Spirit is God in action, manifesting himself in external signs and wonders, and especially in the work of internal witness and recreation.

Now the Spirit in Paul is distinguished both from the Father and from Christ. On that question there can be no doubt. In one passage (II Cor. 3:17) he does, indeed, *seem* to equate the Spirit and the Lord (the latter term he usually reserves for Christ). But the meaning of this verse is *not* that Christ and the Spirit are identical, but that, in his exegesis of an Old Testament verse (Exod. 34:34), Paul understands the "Lord" there referred to, as the Spirit. When he says, "The Lord is the Spirit" (R.S.V.), Paul means, "The word 'Lord' in that passage is to be taken of the Spirit." In what way, then, are Spirit and Christ distinguished?

Christ, as we have already seen, means in Paul a heavenly being in "the form of God," who became incarnate and after his obedient submission to the death of the cross was raised by God to a yet higher, more exalted status (Phil. 2:5 ff.). In Col. 1:15 ff. Paul goes further than this and introduces a theme of the later Logos doctrine, viz., that Christ was the very image of God and the agent of creation. As such, it is hard to see how he could differ from the Spirit—God in action, God expressing himself by his vital energy. Indeed, we may feel that the logic of Paul would, or ought to, have led to his identifying the Spirit and the Christ. How, then, are we to account for the distinction he perpetually observes? A closer look at his doctrine of the Spirit may help to clarify, though not to solve, this difficult issue; for it is evident that Paul had not thought the matter fully through; consequently he introduced some inconsistency into his thinking.

The most revealing verse about the nature of the Spirit in Paul is I Cor. 2:11. There he compares God's Spirit to the spirit within a man, and makes the analogy that as a man's spirit knows a man's thoughts within him, so God's Spirit comprehends God's thoughts. From this it is clear that he thinks of God's Spirit as a good deal more than his dynamic energy, or the means of his operation. It is not merely God's breath, but his self-awareness, his mind, his inner being. This may be the source or seat of God's vitality, but it is more. It is his self-consciousness, his very being, the center of his "person," as we might say. Just as a man's spirit is his ultimate reality, when he is stripped of all that is accidental to his being, so God's Spirit is his inner self. Spirit therefore contrasts with Christ, insofar as the latter is God's image, while the former is his inner being.

But Paul does not stop there. He introduces yet another theme, which is really incongruous with this. In Rom. 8:26 ff., he deals with the Spirit as if he were an entity distinct from the Father, standing over against him and having a mind of his own. The Spirit, says Paul, interecedes for us in prayer; and God, who searches men's hearts, knows what is the "mind" of the Spirit, because the Spirit intercedes in accordance with God's will. Thus the Spirit here, far from being God's inner self, is distinguished from this. He is a heavenly "power" of God—over against the Father—with a mind of his own and operating in the Christian heart.

There is no way to draw together these diverse themes in Paul. In one the Spirit is identical with God's being, in the other he stands over against it. The fact is that Paul has put forward ideas which do not fully harmonize. What, however, may be said further is this: In one sense the Spirit, as God's inner being, is identical with the Father and as such clearly distinguishable from Christ. In the other sense the Spirit is a heavenly power whereby we are aided in our prayers and feel God himself is praying within us. This comes very close to being the same thing as the indwelling Christ. Indeed, Paul attributes to the exalted Christ no less than to the Spirit, this work of intercession (Rom. 8:34). Here the distinction might at first seem to be one in which Christ intercedes for us as removed from the earthly scene and seated at God's right hand, while the Spirit's intercession is associated with his indwelling in the Christian heart. Such a contrast, however, does not fit Paul's viewpoint, since in him Christ, no less than the Spirit, is also indwelling. The distinction in John whereby the Spirit fulfills the place of Jesus, because he has gone away, and acts as Paraclete and Consoler in his absence (John 16), is not entirely Pauline. Indeed, Paul never resolves the issue of the contrast between Christ and the Spirit; and the fact that his characteristic phrase "in Christ" is really synonymous with his other phrase "in the Spirit," betrays the lack of a careful distinction.

At a later time the second and third persons of the Trinity were differentiated in terms of object and subject. The Christ was viewed as God's objective revelation, the Spirit as the means of our subjective appropriation of this. We call Christ "Lord" *in* the Spirit. This distinction will have to be examined in a later chapter, but it is clear that such a limitation of the Spirit's activity is artificial and not true to the biblical witness. It is only one aspect—a favorite one in Paul, to be sure, but still only *one* aspect—of the wider manifestations of the Spirit, which are objective no less than subjective. The Spirit is responsible for signs and wonders, as well as for the internal witness to God's revelation.

Another attempt has recently been made to define the distinction thus: the Spirit is the "agent of revelation," the "quickening cause," while Christ is the "objective ground of salvation" and the "content of the quickened life." [5] While some texts may be exegeted to yield this contrast, it is not possible to apply such a rule generally. To separate "content" from "agency" is really impossible. When the Spirit produces his gifts in the Christian life (Gal. 5:22 ff.), are we to say he is only the agent, while the content of the gifts is not his? When the Spirit speaks within the persecuted Christian as he witnesses to his Lord (Matt. 10:20), are we to say the content of the message is not provided by him? Such reasoning becomes highly sophistical and artificial. Had Paul or other New Testament writers such a distinction in mind, they surely would have been clearer about it, and not written with such ambiguity. The fact of the matter is that the symbolism in the New Testament is still in a fluid state, and no well-defined doctrine has emerged. The Spirit is God's vital energy in a variety of ways, and is not clearly and sharply differentiated from the Christ with any uniform demarcation.

One final question about the Spirit must now be raised. Is the Spirit *personal* in the New Testament? This issue has long been debated and given various answers. The difficulty really lies in what we mean by "personal." Perhaps the matter is best

[5] Lionel S. Thornton, *The Incarnate Lord* (London: Longmans, Green & Co., Ltd., 1928), pp. 322 ff.

put in terms like these: the Spirit is God's active approach to us. Where the Spirit operates, there God himself is at work. The Spirit is not a "thing," over against God, but a way of expressing God in his relation to us. A distinction, to be sure, is implied in that God's breath is not exactly identical with his being, any more than his finger or hand is. Just as we can distinguish our breath or word from ourselves—and yet is it by means of our breath or word that we as selves become selves in relation to others, so the symbolism of God's word or breath is used to indicate God's relation to us. Where the Spirit is given a personal quality as teaching, revealing, witnessing, interceding, creating, and so on, it is not as an entity distinct from God, but as God himself doing these things and yet not compromising his transcendence. To be "in the Spirit," in the Pauline phrase, means to be possessed by God—the metaphor of "in" being taken from demon possession (cf. Mark 1:23, when the demoniac is "*in* an unclean spirit").

This point of view leads to two possible ways of expressing the matter—the two which we have already found foreshadowed in Paul. On the one hand the Spirit can be conceived as God's inner being itself, since it is God who is doing these things. On the other hand, since God is wholly transcendent, the Spirit can in some sense be contrasted with him, for his presence in and around us does not exhaust his being. The paradox of his beyondness and his relatedness is ever with us. Hence Paul can think of the Spirit as a kind of heavenly power with a mind and identity of his own. Such a way of conceiving of the Spirit stems from the desire to guard God's transcendent glory.

We conclude, therefore, that in the New Testament the Spirit is God's dynamic activity expressing itself in a great variety of ways, objective as well as subjective. Sometimes it is thought of as identical with God's inner being, sometimes it is distinguished from the Father as a heavenly power whereby he operates and comes into relation with his world. Behind such a distinction lies the need to contrast God's beyondness with his relatedness; and as expressive of this second aspect of the paradox of God's being, the Spirit is logically identical with the Logos. In the New Testament, however, the Spirit is not identified with the Christ. The distinction between them is variously conceived, dependent upon the underlying Christology in each case. The Spirit can be contrasted with the "Spirit-man," endowed at baptism or conceived in the virgin's womb. But where the Christ is seen to be the incarnate Word himself, then the distinction becomes harder to draw; for the Word fulfills precisely the place of the Spirit, as God in his active relation to the world.

CHAPTER IV

THE TRINITY OF MEDIATION

From our brief study of the New Testament material it has become apparent that the symbols Father, Son, and Spirit do not constitute a genuine Trinity. Not only are the terms themselves ambiguous and have reference to somewhat differing things as New Testament thought develops, but the distinction especially between the Son and the Spirit remains vague and uncertain. Later church thought inherited these symbols; and with its somewhat rigid view of the inspiration of the Scriptures, it was forced to work out its doctrine within their context. In order to be coherent, it was impossible to unify into a single whole the diverse trends of New Testament thinking. In consequence, the doctrines of the Trinity which emerged involved delineating the terms according to the basic structure which was presupposed. This involved some artificiality, as far as it was contended that any doctrine was genuinely scriptural. But the basic problem which faced all such doctrines was the threefold element to which they were confined. Here the major artificiality is to be found, and as we survey the various patterns of trinitarian thinking, this will become clear. While in every case a vital Christian concern was involved, the fact that it had to be expressed within the structure of these symbols, and especially within their threefoldness, gave the consequent doctrines an arbitrary character and posed for them a row of insoluble problems, on which some of the most subtle thinking in Christianity has been done.

The first doctrine of the Trinity we must examine is that which makes the basic distinction between Father and Son, one of mediation. The Son is the Logos, by means of which God comes into relation with this world. What lies behind this idea?

It may be well to begin this discussion with a quotation from Tertullian, who was one of the first to wrestle seriously with the Logos doctrine in Christianity. In his book against Marcion (2:27) he writes:

> Whatever attributes you [i.e., Marcion] require as worthy of God, must be found in the Father, who is invisible and unapproachable, and placid and (so to say) the God of the philosophers; whereas those qualities which you censure as unworthy must be supposed to be in the Son, who has been seen, and heard, and encountered, the Witness and Servant of the Father, uniting in Himself man and God, God in mighty deeds, in weak ones man, in order that He may give to man as much as He takes from God. What in your esteem is the entire disgrace of my God, is in fact the pledge of man's salvation.

The point of this in the actual controversy with Marcion need not concern us. What is of crucial importance to notice is that the Father for Tertullian is the "God of the philosophers"—the Absolute in his self-sufficient and impassible and invisible nature. However unsatisfactory the symbol Father may be for such an idea, Tertullian does not hesitate to make himself clear on the point. The Son, on the other hand, is the one who is seen, heard, and encountered; and by his union with human nature he effects man's salvation. The Son is thus the mediating principle between the Absolute and the world. Elsewhere he expresses it thus: "We must understand the Father as invisible in virtue of the fulness of his majesty, while we recognize the Son as visible in accordance with the measure of a secondary nature" (*Adv. Prax.* 14). The Son is thus distinguished by his secondary rank, because the Son is the one by whom the Father is declared, made known, and encountered. To the Son belong the theophanies of the Old Testament precisely because it is the quality of the Son to manifest God. (This point is treated very fully by Novatian in his tractate on the Trinity, Chs. 17 ff.)

Now, in this early period of Christian thought the full implications of this position were not drawn out. There was a tendency to view the Son as inferior to the Father, and while sharing his Godhead, to have been begotten in a moment of time. "There was a time," says Tertullian, "when the Son was not . . . who made the Lord a Father" (*Adv. Hermog.* 3, 18). Such a position was unsatisfactory, since it really implied an infinite number of mediators. If God the Father is the Absolute, and the Son is begotten in a moment of time, this implies a change in the absolute character of God and also involves the idea that it is not God himself who creates and redeems, but some secondary and inferior mediator. That, indeed, was the position finally of Arius, who held the Logos was a creature and there was a "time" when he was not. (Arius stated this with subtilty, saying, "there was where he was not," to avoid the idea that the earthly, temporal sequence could be applied to the process of the creation of the Word). But Athanasius rightly replied that if the Logos was not fully God, if he was not *eternally* begotten of the Father, an infinite series of mediators was necessary; and, indeed, even with an infinite series we should never be able to reach back to the Absolute. If the Unoriginate could not endure to create creatures because of his absolute character, and so created the Logos to create them, then he equally could not endure to create the Logos. There would infinitely be the need for a mediator: "a Mediator being ever in request, creation will never be constituted" (*De Decr.* 8).

It is from those considerations that the doctrine of the eternal begetting of the Son came to be affirmed. It had been foreshadowed by earlier writers with their efforts to distinguish God's Word as eternally resident in him and then later put forth or uttered for creation (Tertullian *Adv. Prax.* 5), but it was first given clear expression in Origen, who argued that God could not ever have failed to beget his wisdom, for this would imply a defect in the One. Either he was unable to or unwilling to—both of which we must deny (*De Princ.* 1:2:2). Hence the eternal begetting of the Son is a necessary doctrine.

There are two real problems with his approach. There is, in the first place, the assumption that somehow the first term of the Trinity is more really God than the second. Despite the idea of eternal generation, it is true that the Father is the source of the Son: the latter owes his divinity to the former. Novatian puts it very bluntly: "There is one true God and one alone, his (i.e., the Son's) Father." (31). Throughout Greek theology this concern for the Father's arche, as the beginning, the source, the cause of all, from whom the Son and Spirit derive their very being (John of Damascus, *Exp. Fid.* 7), has involved the implicit assumption that God in his relations with the world is secondary to his essential being. Some theologians later on were more careful in this regard. Calvin, for instance, explicitly denies that the Son owes his divinity to the Father. "We pronounce it a detestable figment, that the essence belongs exclusively to the Father, as though he were the author of the Deity of the Son." The Father is only "the original and fountain of the whole Divinity" insofar as he is the author of the *person* of the Son, not of his essential being (*Instit.* 1:13:24-5). This Calvin can say, being a child of Western thinking on the Trinity, which we shall examine in the next section. But it seriously raises the question of how Father and Son can be distinguished in terms of begetting, since it denies the basic difference on which all the earlier thinking rested.

The second problem of this Trinity of mediation is the assumption that the Absolute can beget the mediator. Of this I have already treated, and I have pointed out that it stems from the attempt to compose an essential paradox. It goes back to the idea of the fecundity of the Absolute, which by its overflowing nature produces the Logos and, in turn, the world. But this is to deny the very quality of the Absolute, which cannot have anything left "over," and which ever stands in a paradoxical relation to the world. Every attempt to do justice to the absolute character of God cannot overcome this paradox; and every attempt to relate his beyondness to his relatedness is doomed to failure by the very nature of these terms. If the one is in any sense begotten of the other, then the other is no longer absolute. The result of deriving God in his visible and encountered nature from God in his invisibility and self-sufficiency is to compromise the latter. We have reached the confines of human thought; and in our need to do justice both to God's absolute transcendence and to his being in relation, we can say no more than that we hold both these things to be true. Both are vital for Christian faith; but the one is not derived from the other. God is not God in any secondary or inferior sense because of his capacity for relations. He is God in these two ways, of which neither is prior, neither primary.

One further implication of this Trinity of mediation must now engage us in this connection: it is the idea that the Son is nearer to suffering than the Father. This is the issue of Patripassianism (the suffering of the Father) in the early Church, and it has always played an important role in the effort to distinguish Father and Son. It is one aspect of the attempt to deal with the unchangeable nature of God and his being involved in the flux and change and consequent suffering of the world.

There were those in the early Church who identified the Father and the Son, and we shall examine their ideas under the section dealing with the Trinity of revelation. Here we are concerned with the answer made to them by the Logos theologians. In essence it was that their opponents made the Father suffer—they "crucified God the Father," as Tertullian bluntly put it (*Adv. Prax.* 1). The implication is that in some sense the Son suffers, while the Father does not. Seeing, however, that by definition the divine essence which the Son shares with the Father is impassible, how could the Son's suffering be fitly stated? Tertullian in wrestling with the problem in a passage which is most unclear (*Adv. Prax.* 29), at least is clear in this; that "the Spirit of God [i.e., in Christ] suffered nothing in its own name," although the Son suffered in his humanity. This was put more cogently by Cyril of Alexandria much later: The Son "was in his crucified body impassibly making his own the sufferings of his own flesh" (3rd Ep. to Nestorius). That is to say, the Son is able to appropriate suffering in a way the Father cannot. Granted there is a paradox in saying he appropriates it impassibly, still the distinction between Father and Son is clear at this point, that it is the Son and not the Father who does the appropriating, and the Father's absolute character is thus guarded.

Now, it is essential to say these two things about God, viz., that he is beyond suffering and dwells in unspeakable joy, and yet he participates in human suffering and by this participation both reveals his character as love and reclaims fallen humanity. This is the very center of the Christian mystery, that redemptive suffering is the quality of God. The Cross stands at the heart of Christianity; and a God who is only impassible is not the God of the Christians. We are driven thus to formulate a paradox—God is joy, yet he suffers; and this is one more aspect of the basic paradox of God's beyondness and his relatedness. We have to say both and leave it at that. We can, to be sure, understand to a limited extent in our own lives that joy and suffering are related. Our capacity for deep joy does depend upon the extent of our sympathy and the amount we ourselves have suffered and are able to suffer in and for others. Yet in applying these terms to God, we cannot avoid paradoxical statements. The creature is not the creator; and the relation we can observe between joy and suffering has something to do with our being creatures, and fallen creatures at that. Somehow we have to say that God is complete joy, and yet he takes to himself the suffering born of sin. This is the character of God: he exists in these two ways, these two modes of being. But neither is derived from the other; and we must positively refuse to say that as *begotten* the Word stands nearer to suffering, as if this were a defect, than does the Father. It is the derivative principle in the Trinity of mediation which is here so misleading. It is not because he is begotten of the Father that the Son stands in a relation to suffering in which the Father does not; rather God's joy and suffering are essential antinomies of his nature.

One final question must now engage us in connection with

the Trinity of mediation, and that is the sense in which the terms can be personalized. What was meant when Father and Son were contrasted as two persons or "hypostases"?

It may be wise to interject at this point that we are dealing with only two principles, the Father and the Son. The question of the place of the Spirit in the Trinity is reserved for another chapter. In the early thinking, while the Spirit played a distinct role, he was not really essential to the Trinity, his place being logically identical with that of the Logos. It was not till Augustine worked out the idea of the Spirit as the uniting bond between Father and Son—something indeed which is hinted at earlier, e.g., Athenag. *Plea* 10, but not developed—that a genuine ontology of the threefoldness of the Trinity emerged. For my purposes in this section I may merely remark that the idea of the Logos as God in his active relations with the world, covers all that can be said of the Holy Spirit. If the latter is the inspirer of the prophets, sanctifier, hallower, internal witness, and so on—the chief ways in which he is thought of in the early fathers—he cannot really be distinguished from the Logos. For the inward work of inspiration and sanctification is not *in principle* different from any of the other manifold forms in which God is at work in the world. We can, indeed, distinguish a large variety of ways in which God operates, but no necessity drives us to regard them in two such distinct categories that we are justified thereby in distinguishing the Logos and the Spirit in terms of their operations. It is for this reason that until Augustine the place of the Spirit in the Trinity is unsatisfactory and ambiguous. When, for instance, Justin Martyr can attribute the inspiration of the Scriptures to the Word (*Apol.* 1:36) no less than to the Spirit (1:30-60), and regards the Spirit at the birth of Jesus as none other than the Logos (1:33), he is saying something that is equally applicable to every reference to the Spirit.

To return, then, to our question: What does "person" mean? "Person," or to use the Greek term *hypostasis,* means a distinct entity, standing in contrast to another. In early Christian thinking it is viewed *objectively,* not subjectively. When we think of "person" we tend to think in psychological terms. A person is primarily a center of self-consciousness. But the earlier attitude was the opposite of this. Not self-consciousness, but *confrontation,* was the underlying idea. A person was a *prosopon,* a "facing towards" (as the word literally means in Greek), or a *persona,* a "sounding through" (as it means in the Latin). A person was a discreet entity whom one encountered by looking at him or by hearing him speak. *Persona* thus could mean a mask worn by actors, whereby they confronted the audience with a definite character and expressed this by his words in a play. Father and Son were thus distinguishable in terms, not of self-consciousness, but of presenting a special "face"—a distinct nature, quality, or aspect of being. The term which really best expresses what was intended is that of "mode of being" (*tropos hyparxeōs*). God is known, or inferred, as existing in different modes. As Father he is, as we have seen, absolute; as Son he is related to the world. But in both instances he is the same one God. Hence the modes, clearly and even paradoxically distinguished, share an *identity* of essence. They are both God. One is confronted with two ways in which God exists; neither can be reduced to the other, yet both are God.

The other way of expressing this was to use the Greek term *hypostasis.* This meant "under standing" and referred to the unique and distinct element which underlay a special existence.

It meant the principle of differentiation, by which we "understand" something as different from something else, and which was considered as underlying its mere outward appearance. In its very nature it was a distinct, discreet entity.

These words greatly suffered in their history, and they have caused all sorts of unnecessary confusions. Once we grasp what the Church fathers were trying to say, we shall find this question of "person" and "hypostasis" a rather secondary issue in trinitarian thinking. They were attempting to distinguish two different ways in which God existed—the same God, to be sure, but two different ways or modes of his being God.

Of the confusions of the terms, we must mention first that the Latin equivalent of *hypostasis* was *substantia* (standing under). Now the idea of "standing under" could be taken in two very different senses. It could mean the principle of differentiation as we have shown above; and that is what "hypostasis" came to mean in the orthodox formula of the Trinity, three hypostases and one essence or *ousia*. But it could also mean the fundamental essence behind the two modes of God's being. It could mean the underlying reality of the modes—the being of God itself. That is what the Latins meant by *substantia,* when they contrasted three persons and one substance. There is no wonder, therefore, that church debates were often beclouded by the issue, since the same term, in its Greek and Latin equivalents, was being used in radically different senses.

A second confusion is one which concerns the issue whether God's underlying essence, the reality of God beneath the modes of his being, is generic or particular. If it is generic, the danger of tritheism is obvious. If the Father and the Son share a common essence, they in no way differ from the gods of polytheism, who all shared a common divinity. Thus the divinity was divided up among many gods. Now some of the Cappadocian fathers in the fourth century did not completely avoid this danger. Basil, particularly, tends at times to contrast hypostasis and *ousia* in terms of the particular and the general (Ep. 38:2; 214:4). There are three discreet realities which share a common divinity. But this is far from the whole of his thought, and in Ep. 52 he gives a much more orthodox statement of the matter. However this may be, what the Cappadocians really meant and finally clearly said, was that the three hypostases shared an *identity* of essence. There were not three gods with a common divinity, but one God with three modes of his being (see Gregory of Nyssa, *On "Not Three Gods"*). The three in the Godhead are not marked by individual circumscription, as are three men who share a common humanity. Rather the three of the Trinity act together by their mutual interpenetration, and what in any given instance they effect is not three *separate* things (as the ancient gods did separate things often in conflict with one another), but is the *same* thing. The life from God is not three separate things from three life-givers, but one and the same life. This doctrine of the mutual interpenetration or coinherence of the Trinity was later called the "perichōresis," in the sense that the persons moved within each other and contained each other (from *chorein,* to move or contain).

What then was being stated in the classical doctrine of the Council of Constantinople of A.D. 381, was that God existed in three distinct modes, but these modes had an *identity* of being. This, of course, is a paradoxical statement, for how can there be diverse modes if there is an identity of being? It is merely the statement of a necessary paradox that the one God exists as both beyond and related, inaccessible and encountered. As such a statement it is more or less adequate. The difficulty, however, arises—as we have seen—from trying to derive one mode from the other.[1]

It is true that after the Arian controversy the sharp contrast between the Father as the Absolute and the Son as God in his relations with the world, was partly modified. The distinction is more between the Father as the uncaused source of all being, and the Son as the actualizer of creation. This modification was partly due to the influence of the biblical witness in which the Father is not solely the remote and transcendent deity, but also has a direct relation with his world. It was also due to the fact that the overemphasis by Arius on the Father as the transcendent God, had led to his thinking of the Son as distinctly inferior. To challenge this inferiority, Athanasius and the Cappadocians brought the Father into a closer relation with the world. Yet behind the distinction of source and actualizer there really lay the older contrast between the Absolute and the Mediator, though there was a definite toning down of the sharpness of the antithesis. Athanasius, unlike Tertullian, could never have spoken of the Father as the "God of the philosophers." That would have sounded like Arianism. Of Gregory of Nyssa's view I shall treat later under the section on the Trinity of God's activity.

Such, then, is the doctrine of the Trinity of mediation. A recent statement of it is given by Karl Barth in his *Doctrine of the Word of God,* Vol. I, pp. 349 ff., especially pp. 363 ff. He deals with the question, to be sure, in terms solely of revelation, and posits the basic distinction as one of God as veiled and hidden,

[1] The problem of the third term in the Trinity will engage us in Chapter VI.

over against his being unveiled and manifest. He contends the one is derived from the other, since it is God's most esssential characteristic that "His nature cannot be unveiled to man."[2] Yet "the fact of His revelation declares that it is His property to distinguish Himself from Himself, i.e. in Himself and hiddenly to be God and yet at the same time in quite another way, namely, manifestly, i.e. in the form of something He Himself is not, to be God a second time."[3] Now this distinction is, in terms of revelation, the fundamental, paradoxical distinction with which we have been confronted throughout this discussion; and Barth's contention of the derivation of God's revealed mode of being from his hidden mode of being, is open to the same objections we have already made with regard to the Logos doctrine.

It may be added that while Barth has done more than any other modern theologian to restore the doctrine of the Trinity to a place of first rank in Christian dogmatics, his treatment is open not only to the objections we have raised, but also to a further one, viz., that this basic distinction is not carried through in his treatment of the doctrine of God as Father.[4] There he deals with God as creator, where logic should have driven him to deal primarily with God as *completely* hidden and remote, which he certainly is not in creation. Barth does, to be sure, introduce the doctrine of appropriations,[5] which I shall deal with in a later section; and he contends that the whole Trinity, and not the Father only, is involved in creation, and that it is only by "appropriation" that we attribute this work to the Father

[2] Barth, *op. cit.*, p. 362.
[3] *Ibid.*, p. 363.
[4] *Ibid.*, pp. 441 ff.
[5] *Ibid.*, pp. 428 ff.

alone, because he is "antecedently Father in Himself," i.e., of the Son.[6] That is to say, we refer to the one person what is really characteristic of the three, because there is a special appropriateness in this, since the Father is originator of the Son; and the idea of origination in creation leads us to think of the one who is originator in the highest possible sense. But all this spells an element of confusion. Behind it lies the idea of the Father as really more God than the Son, as antecedently God, and as the real cause of all things (though Barth is as vigorous in his objections to these inferences as he is unpersuasive in overcoming them). Moreover, to treat the concept "Father" *exclusively* under the category of "Creator" is really to abandon the basic distinction of unveiled and veiled and to relate the Father so closely to creation that he loses that absolute character implied in his being truly "unveiled." If we set up the basic trinitarian distinction in terms of transcendence, hiddenness, and beyondness on the one hand, and relation, unveiling on the other, we shall find the symbols Father and Son peculiarly inappropriate for this, and we shall have to deal with all God's relatedness—in creation, redemption, and so forth—under the category of the Son, not of the Father. The "appropriations" only becloud this issue. It is the ambiguity of the symbols which leads to this confusion. The paradox of God's beyondness and his relatedness cannot fittingly be expressed in this way, for the term Father is a term of relationship, and in its Hebrew background and in the teaching of Jesus refers to God's direct relation with his world.

Our conclusion, then, concerning the Trinity of mediation is this: the terms Father and Son are unfitting to express God

[6] *Ibid.*, p. 450.

in his beyondness over against God in his relations with the world. Not only are the symbols inadequate, seeing that Father itself is a term of relationship, but also the assumption that the one is in any way derived from the other is unwarranted and tries vainly to compose an essential paradox. That the basic distinction *must* be made, and that it can fittingly be spoken of in terms of two "modes of being" in God, we have attempted to show. That, furthermore, a third term is necessary to the other two, so that a Trinity is thus found in God, is very open to question. For all that can be said of the Spirit is really implicit in the Logos; and, indeed, it is partly[7] for that reason that no true and distinctive place was found for the Spirit in early Christian thinking. If one sets up the primary distinction in terms of beyondness and relatedness, of veiling and unveiling, no third term is necessary. There is an antinomy, a paradox—no more. A third term emerges in different structures of thought, to which I must now turn. In what sense it is valid there, I shall have to discuss. But it is patent that it can play no proper role in a Trinity (or rather a duality), in which the primary terms are the contrast between the absolute and relative character of God. Once we have agreed there is no possible way by which to bring these terms in relationship, since by their very nature they are self-contradictory, we shall not be led to find a third term or some principle of derivation by which to unite them. The Spirit as the uniting bond of the Trinity (an idea to be examined in Augustine later) makes no sense whatever when the first two terms are defined as paradoxical. The fact, for

[7] Not *wholly,* of course, since it is possible, though not particularly cogent, to regard the Spirit as the uniting bond of the Trinity, if the Logos is viewed as *derived* from the Absolute (see Athenag., *Plea* 10).

instance, which has often been a starting point for considering the distinctive role of the Spirit—that God operates *subjectively* in us, as well as presenting us *objectively* with his creation and revelation—cannot be made to reflect some third mode of being in God, distinct from the basic paradox with which we began. It can only be understood as one of the variety of ways in which God comes into relation with his world, and so it is implicit in the second term—God in his relatedness.

CHAPTER V

THE TRINITY OF LOVE

THE ATTEMPT TO UNDERSTAND THE FATHER AND THE SON OF THE Trinity in terms of the Greek Absolute or of God's final transcendence over against his relatedness, could never be satisfactory to a theology oriented toward the Scriptures. There the intimate relation of the Father with his world was too clear to make such a delimitation of the first two terms cogent. In consequence, the doctrine of the Trinity developed along somewhat different lines. The idea of the Father as remote and inaccessible in distinction to the Son who could become visible and encountered, seemed to endanger their essential equality. It suggested the inferiority of the Son, as Arius had propounded it. To overcome this difficulty it was now argued that the Father no less than the Son could "appear" and be made manifest. This is a point of great consequence in Augustine's treatment of the Trinity, and it emerges with clarity in his discussion of the Old Testament theophanies. He contends that an appearance of the Father is no less possible than one of the Son. Because the persons of the Trinity share the same divine essence, there can be no distinction on that score. Indeed, the visit of the three men, who appeared to Abraham in Gen. 18, is an indication of this equality. The three men "visibly intimated by the visible creature, the equality of the Trinity, and one and the same substance in three persons" (*De Trin*. 2. 11. 20). Similarly, in interpreting Dan. 7:9-11,

Augustine concludes from the vision of the Ancient of days that "it is not, therefore, unsuitably believed that God the Father also was wont to appear to mortals" (2. 18. 33). Such appearances do not imply, of course, that God manifests himself "as he properly is." The Father's nature in itself, no less than the Son's, is invisible. But in both cases, God makes "intimations of himself to mortal senses by a corporeal form and likeness" (2. 18. 35). In the Father's case he makes use of angelic forms in some way (3. 11. 21-2), while of course in the incarnation of the Son there is the assumption of the human flesh. The fundamental point, however, is that Father and Son are not to be distinguished in terms of the absolute and the related.

How then are they to be differentiated? Why is there a Father over against the Son? There are in Augustine and in the later Roman Catholic theology two answers to this. On the one hand the Father is regarded as the principle of divinity, the source and cause of everything: from him the Son is begotten. On the other hand the distinctions within the Godhead are a necessity because God is love. If he loves and if he is self-sufficient and independent of his creation, he must have an object of his love different from his creatures. If he can only love his creatures and is dependent upon them to express his love, he would no longer be truly God. Hence the Father loves the Son.

Now, these are really two quite different ideas, by no means necessarily related. The treatment of them as if they were inseparably combined, is largely the consequence of the whole tradition that Augustine inherited. The distinction between Father and Son in terms of source or cause, is one which goes back to the attempt to relate the Absolute to the world by the principle of God's fecundity. The Father overflows with his being and so produces first the distinctions in the Godhead and then finally the created existence. The difficulties with this view have already been examined sufficiently. What is important here to stress is that the original contrast between the Absolute and the Related, between the Veiled and the Unveiled, has been so toned down that one can reasonably ask why the distinction between Father and Son in this connection is any longer important. If it is not to guard the Father's absolute transcendence that there is a Son, why should there be a Son?

"The Father," says Augustine, "is the beginning of the whole divinity, or if it is better so expressed, of the deity" (4. 20. 29). Or, to quote a modern Roman Catholic treatment:

> To the Father, indeed, the ineffable name of God belongs preeminently, since he is the principle of the whole divinity, since divinity pours forth from Him to the other two persons.
>
> He is the source of Being, of all being, actually existing or conceivable, in God or outside of God. Within God He is the principle of existence. Outside of God, He is the cause of existence. He is the necessary Being, eternal, absolute, from whom all things come, on whom all things depend.[1]

Now, the question to be asked is this: if the Father is the Absolute and comes into relation by the Son, we are back again at the basic paradoxical distinction which has so much concerned us. But if on the other hand, because of the weight of the biblical tradition and the ambiguous nature of the term Father, he can in some sense have a direct relation with the world and

[1] Felix Klein, *The Doctrine of the Trinity,* tr. Daniel J. Sullivan (New York: P. J. Kenedy & Sons, 1940), p. 109.

appear in the theophanies, he is no longer the Absolute. The idea that the Father is the source of being is a remnant of the old idea that the Absolute is at the same time the source of all, by its fecundity and overflowing nature. But if the absolute character of the Father is no longer really absolute, the idea that he is the source of all being, and thereby to be distinguished from the Son, does not make much sense. For the fundamental distinction is abandoned, and there is really no need for a second principle in the Godhead. The Father himself is both absolute and related. As such he is both source of being and "being" in relationship.

This has always been a problem in this tradition of thinking about the Trinity, and the inherent difficulty is evident in a consideration of two fundamental aspects of the Western doctrine. These concern the "missions" in regard to the persons of the Trinity, and the conviction that in their exterior operations the persons of the Trinity are indistinguishable (*opera trinitatis ad extra indivisa sunt:* the external actions of the Trinity are undivided). Let us consider these, taking the second first.

THE APPROPRIATIONS AND THE MISSIONS

In any divine operation, it is argued, the *whole* Trinity is at work; and it is at work in such a way that we cannot say that one event belongs to the Father and another to the Son, nor that one *aspect* of a given event belongs to the Father and another to the Son. To make such distinctions would be to compromise the simplicity of the divine essence which all three persons share and are. All three are *equally* and *indistinguishably* involved in all events. If we say the Father does "this," while the Son does "that," we are not speaking literally and properly. The only fitting thing to say is that the Trinity does *both* this and that. God operates as one. Hence, in the Lord's Prayer, when we say, "Our Father," our address is *not* to the Father alone, but to the Trinity (Aug. De Trin. 5. 11. 12). Similarly, in the incarnation *all* the three persons are involved (2. 5. 9), just as in the baptism of Jesus (4. 21. 30) and in the beginning of creation (5. 13. 14). Any distinctions in these operations of God would imply a schism in the simple, divine essence.

Why, then, do we sometimes say, the Father does this, while the Son does that, as if some external act were the prerogative of one of the persons alone? Only by speaking loosely and metaphorically. Such statements, as the Scriptures make them, must not be taken at their face value. They are symbolic, not literal. Yet they are important to make, though they may be misleading if we do not fully appreciate what we are doing. Indeed, they are not only important to make but also necessary to make, in order to draw our attention to the fact that there is a Trinity. Without making them we should be in danger of neglecting the doctrine of the Trinity altogether. What then do we mean by making these distinctions where none really exist? We mean to draw attention to the fact that in some divine event there is a *similarity* between a main feature of this event and some one of the relations within the Godhead. It is only a similarity; it does not mean that only the one person is involved in the event or in its main feature. If, for instance, we see somewhere the revelation of God's omnipotence, we have a right to say: this is the *Father* doing something. In literal truth it is the *whole* Trinity doing something, but the omnipotent character of the event makes us think of the Father as the source of all, the final principle of being. So we say the Father is at work there, not literally but by "appropriation." We appropriate this event to him (though it really belongs equally and indivisibly to the whole Trinity), because it reminds us of the special quality of the Father in the internal relations of the Godhead. There, as we have seen, he is the absolute source of being. Hence an event which discloses his awful power, although an event of the whole Trinity, is appropriated to the Father to remind us of his special character. If, again, we think of creation, we can say that the decree to create is the Father's; the execution of the decree, the Son's; the perfecting of the work, the Spirit's. But it is not literally this way. All three persons are equally involved in all three aspects of creation. But in each case the distinction points us to a real distinction *within* the Godhead and suggests what we must think about when we think about the Trinity, although the distinction does *not* belong to the events we are describing. These merely suggest it, hint at it. We talk in metaphors, rather than literally.

This is the Roman doctrine of the "appropriations." There are distinctions of internal relations *within* the Trinity, but these are not characterized by any distinctions of their *external* operation. Events may suggest to our minds a similarity between them and the different persons; but it is only a similarity. The divine essence operates as one.

Now this idea is not fully cogent. While it is a necessity once the distinction between Father and Son as the Absolute over against the related is abandoned, it does not really do justice to the distinction which still remains. For if the Father is the source of all, then obviously in any given event he is literally to be distinguished from the Son as its absolute source. While the Son may play some role in the event, he certainly cannot play *that* role. Yet that is what we are forbidden to say by the doctrine of the appropriations. The fact of the matter is that the idea of the Father as the absolute source and yet as not entirely absolute but in some way as related, has confused the original distinction between Father and Son, and has left the way by which we can differentiate them uncertain and ambiguous.

This becomes particularly clear in dealing with the incarnation. Why is the Son and not the Father incarnate? The early answer to that question was very simple—viz., the Father is the Absolute; the Son, God-in-Relations. Hence, to guard God's final transcendence, the Son, not the Father, is said to be incarnate. To say the latter is to fall into the error of Patripassianism, to imply that the Father suffers. The Son stands in a closer relation to suffering than the Father, precisely because the Son is God as he relates himself to his world. But once this distinction is abandoned, no reason can be found why the Son and not the Father becomes incarnate. On the doctrine of the appropriations the logic would be to say all *three* persons were incarnate, and we appropriate this to the Son, as suggestive of his being begotten of the Father in the internal relations of the divine life. But the Scriptures forbid us to say that. The Son and not the Father became incarnate. The most that Augustine dare say about this is that the whole Trinity was involved in the incarnation insofar as they were all *equally* at work in the creation of the manhood of Jesus ("The Trinity wrought together the flesh of the Son," 4. 21. 30) and in the "sending" of the Son (2. 5. 9). But it was the Son and not the Father who was sent and became incarnate.

Facing the same issue, Anselm has to argue that the Son and not the Father became incarnate because the Son had suffered a special affront from the devil when the latter had set himself up in the "likeness" of God, which is the special prerogative of the Son. The argument is not very convincing, since there was an even greater affront to the Father in the devil's action. Or again, Anselm argued, if the Father had become incarnate, this would have involved a series of possible "grandsons" in the Trinity. The Father would be the grandson of the Virgin's parents, and the Word would be the grandson of the Virgin, since he is the real Son of the Father (*Cur Deus Homo?* 9)! Anselm resorts to these incredible arguments precisely because he dare not introduce the Patripassian theme, since the basic distinction on which it rested was no longer held.

Augustine wrestles manfully with the question under the terms, "Why is the Son *sent?*" The answer should have been simple: the Son is "sent" because the Father is the Absolute, while the Son is God in relation. But having related the Father to the world in the Old Testament theophanies, Augustine well knows such an answer is impossible. Sending would imply the very inferiority of the Son, which he wishes to challenge. Hence he never really answers the question. He tries to read out of the term "sent" every vestige of subordinationism, contending the operation involves all the three persons and merely entails "making . . . visible"—exhibiting and presenting to mortal eyes (2. 5. 9-10)—something which characterizes even the Father as visible in the theophanies. And yet Scripture never says the Father is sent. Why not? Because, says Augustine, the expression would be inappropriate since it implies derivation, and the Father "has no one of whom to be, or from whom to proceed" (4. 20. 28). But if this is true of the Father, does not this really vitiate Augustine's whole argument? Is not the Son sent precisely because he is second to the Father, as derived from the Absolute, and thus able to come into relations with the world in a way the Father cannot?

The Roman Catholic doctrine of the "missions" is founded on this confusion in Augustine. Most Catholic theologians make a sharp distinction between the missions and the appropriations. Writes Klein:

> The missions (or "sendings") are of another order altogether. They express the workings in relation to temporal effects of the eternal properties peculiar to the Person sent; they communicate to us the gifts and graces which correspond to them; they are truly related to the origin of the divine Persons, with what distinguishes Them within the Trinity.[2]

But why it is the Son and not the Father who is sent, is never made clear. As we have already observed, the logic of the appropriations would be to regard the *whole* Trinity as incarnate, as it is the whole Trinity which is at work in all things equally and indivisibly. The fact of the matter is that the missions are a remnant of the old Absolute-Related distinction inherited from the early church, and can only be upheld by such artificial arguments as Anselm adduces, or by regarding the mystery of the Trinity as revealed and as beyond all human comprehension.

Once the principles of God's absolute transcendence and of his relation to the world are seen to be characteristic of the Father himself, the problem arises, how can Father and Son be distinguished? No longer is it possible to formulate a Trinity (or at any rate a duality) as the basis of the old contrast. How then

[2] P. 212.

can we talk about internal relations within the Godhead? Is it necessary to distinguish them, and what do they mean? It is at this point that the principle of "God is love" is introduced.

GOD AS LOVE

That God is love is the most characteristic affirmation of the Christian gospel; and the work of Jesus Christ is seen precisely in this: God reveals and acts out in terms of history his essential nature as redeeming love. But if God is love, and if it is also necessary to assume that he is independent of the world he creates and redeems, how are we to express this? How are we to think of God in such a way that he does not need the world in order to find an object for his love? That is, how is he love in his essential nature before all worlds and before this particular world of ours?

Christian theology has tried to solve this problem in two different ways. There are those who have pictured God as loving himself, while others have pictured God as in some sense a society. In both cases a Trinity has been conceived. In the first instance a Trinity has been found in an analysis of self-consciousness. God has been conceived as analagous with a single person, in particular a single mind, which in loving itself makes itself objective to itself and loves its own image. In the second instance God has been thought of as more than one person—as three, in fact; but to avoid the obvious dangers of tritheism in such an idea, the nature of these persons and the way they are united into a single whole has been stated in such a manner that they are not really persons in the usual sense of that term. Later on I shall examine both these conceptions and try to show there are values, as well as defects, in both these ways of thinking. It is necessary, for some reasons, to think of God as a single person who loves himself; there are equally weighty but different reasons for thinking of him as in some sense a society. Before embarking on that inquiry, however, it is needful first to discuss the way in which this doctrine of God as love has been related to the issue of God as the Absolute and as coming into relations. Actually, these two problems are not the same; and it is somewhat unfortunate that they have been inseparably related in the classic patterns of trinitarian thinking. They do not belong together, and it is my purpose to try to show how unhappy has been their union and into what difficulties the combining of them has led.

If we consider, first, the problem of the Absolute from the point of view of the paradox of God's modes of being, which I have so much dwelt upon, it will at once be evident that we cannot equate God's beyondness and his relatedness with "persons" in the Godhead, who love one another. Whether we consider these persons from the analogy of a single person loving his own image, or from the analogy of two or three persons loving each other, it really makes no sense to say that God as beyond loves God as related, or God as veiled loves God as unveiled. We are mixing up two different things, two different concerns and sets of symbols. Aspects or modes of being do not love one another. It is persons as centers of self-consciousness, that love one another; and it is quite unnecessary and indeed confusing to deal with two separate issues about the being of God, as if they were the same. It is one thing to ask: how is the problem of the Absolute to be expressed? It is quite another to ask: how can we most fittingly symbolize God as love? When we think of God we are constantly driven to state various antinomies, which it is impossible for us to compose. He is love and he is wrath; he is rest and he is motion; he is joy and yet he in some sense suffers. Yet no one would try to say that his "love" loves his wrath, or his being at rest loves his being in motion. Equally misleading and confusing is it, therefore, to say that his absolute character loves his character as related and revealed.

There is, however, a further objection to be brought against the notion that God's being as absolute loves his being as related. It is that love is a term of union, and it is precisely the paradoxical character of these modes of being in God, which it is important to hold. They are not related to each other in any conceivable way—else they would not be paradoxical. If we try to relate them, we destroy the paradox and sacrifice something essential in each of the terms. We either compromise the divine transcendence or relate God so much to the world that he becomes dependent upon it. The problem of the Absolute involves a necessary contradiction which we can never solve. Hence we must separate this issue and its mode of expression, from the very different issue of the fitting way in which to speak of God as love.

Let us now ask what is involved in thinking about God as love in terms where the paradox of the Absolute and the Related is not used to distinguish Father and Son. We have already seen that under the influence of the biblical tradition of the term Father, the original contrast between Father and Son, as the Absolute and as God in his relations, was overcome. We have observed furthermore that it was the idea of God as love which then came to serve as the principle by which a Trinity in the Godhead could be defended. The Lover loves the Beloved. More than one term in the Godhead is essential in order that God's nature as love can be fittingly expressed. How was this worked out?

It was developed in terms that the Lover loves the one he has begotten. The Father loves the Son. But why, we may ask, does God love one whom he *begets?* Why is the begetting essential to the symbolism of love? Two answers were given to this, and behind them both there still lurks the problem of the Absolute, in one form or another.

So far as God is thought of as one person who loves himself, which is the primary way in which Augustine conceives the problem, the answer is that he loves his word or image. God is essentially the thinker, the divine Mind, who projects himself as a mental image and loves his image. In turn the image loves the source whence he is begotten. What does this involve? It involves the assumption that intellectual categories are the best from which to derive analogies with God, because they represent the highest element in man, and indeed the point at which he is made in God's image. While it is admitted these categories "fall short in the representation of divine objects," yet, because they are characteristic of "the highest creatures," they are most apt. "Now the intellectual nature imitates God chiefly in this, that God understands and loves Himself" (Aquinas, *S. T.* 1.27.1; 1.93.4). In this way Aquinas succinctly clarifies the essential position of Augustine and the Greek inheritance from Philo. I shall leave aside the question of the validity of these analogies for the moment, and ask further about the begetting. It is contended that the very nature of the self is to objectify itself and then to find satisfaction in this objectification. Such would be the modern way of expressing it. Our self-transcendence involves our loving the image of the self. Let us assume there is a right way to do this, as well as a wrong way—that there is a genuine and healthy self-love, as well as a perverted and egocentric kind. It is certainly of the right kind of self-love of which these authors are here speaking. Some kind of basic self-affirmation is essential to love and to proper self-denial. Our relations with ourselves mirror rather accurately our relations with others. The man who hates himself, equally hates others. The one who is a tyrant toward himself, is a tyrant toward his fellows. There is a right self-love, which alone is the true basis of self-sacrifice, just as there is a perverted type, which is egocentric and sinful.

Now, in a human person the image so begotten, the "word" or "logos" (to use the ancient term), is fleeting and ephemeral. It cannot in any sense be called a "person." But in God, it is argued, this is not so. While our speech or logos passes into nonexistence, we cannot think of God's thought of himself as being unsubstantial. "The incorruptible and eternal nature (of God) has a *logos* which is eternal and substantial" (Greg. Nyss. *Cat. Orat.* 1). God's thought of himself, thus, has the same eternal quality he has; it stands eternally over against him. God thus begets of his own mind the one he loves. Both are eternal; and the begotten Word loves its source in return.

There are, however, two problems of no small proportions, which are involved in this way of thinking. On the one hand, the assumption that the distinction between God and his thought is more radical than the distinction between a human being and his thought, is somewhat unwarranted. Why should we suppose that the thought he begets has a more independent subsistence, than in our own case? Should we not rather assume it has less, that God and his thought are so *identical* that they are indistinguishable? The duality implicit in our thought is due to our being creatures. Why should we imagine that in God this duality is even more marked than in ourselves? Long ago Plotinus saw this problem; and while we may rightly criticize many consequences he tried to draw from it, it is hard to reject his contention that it is better to think of God as the One, than as involved in this kind of duality. That God is in some sense a personal God, does not at all imply as a necessary inference that this sharp duality is characteristic of his thinking. If God loves himself, he loves *himself;* and there is nothing more to be said. He does not love his word or image or anything else. He loves himself.

This brings us to the second objection. When a man thinks of himself or loves himself, the duality of his thought does not imply a second "person," so that the projected self or thought can in turn think of him and love him. There is no mutual relation. The idea that because God's thought is eternal, it in turn can think of him and love him, really makes no sense.[3] The analogy has ceased to be an analogy that bears the remotest resemblance to anything characteristic of our intellect. And if we say that this is because we are creatures while he is God, we shall do best to abandon the analogy altogether, since it has ceased to be an analogy. In actual fact, the intellectual categories are not at all essential to symbolizing the way in which God loves himself. They only confuse it. If God loves himself, he loves himself, and not one who is begotten of him. Nor does his thought love him

[3] This confusion is very apparent in Aquinas. By using Boethius' famous definition of "person" as "an individual substance of a rational nature," the mutual relations of love in the Trinity are made possible. But the caution Aquinas attaches to such a definition in claiming it is really inadequate to express the threefold divine life, really cancels this out. For his fundamental doctrine is that of Augustine, whereby the one Person is characterized by the intellectual relations of will and intellect (*S.T.* 1. 29).

in return. These categories had their origin, as shown in an earlier chapter referring to Philo, in the attempt to compose the paradox of the Absolute and the Relative. In that connection they were unsatisfactory; they are even more obviously unsatisfactory in dealing with God's nature as love.

The second answer to the question of the begetting in this connection is put in ontological, rather than intellectual terms. The Godhead is conceived, not from the point of view of God as one person loving himself, but from the point of view of God loving another whom he begets from his being. The persons of the Trinity are real persons and not intellectual relations. But this way of putting the issue is even more untenable than the first. The begetting is understood as the outcome of the fecundity of the Absolute. The Divine overflows and hence begets the Son.

But this is the very assumption which is forbidden, once the paradox of God as absolute and related is understood *not* as distinguishing Father and Son, but as something characteristic of the Father's nature itself. Or again, if the idea is that the Father is the absolute source of being and hence simple, and begets the Son to love him and be loved by him, because love cannot exist in singleness and simplicity, then the problem is: how can the One ever beget? We are back again at the old paradox of the Absolute and the Related. God is *both* simplicity and diversity, the One and the Many. And not only are these not related, the Many not being derived from the One, but also these modes of being in the Godhead are not such that they can love each other.

In short, the idea of the "begetting" bears no necessary relation to the way in which we think of God as love. It is a term which, in one way or another, belongs to the problem of the

Absolute and the Related, and bears no essential connection with this other issue. Furthermore, behind all the Christian use of the term there lurks another confusion—viz., that between the relation of the heavenly Father to the man Jesus, and the necessary distinction to be made in the Godhead. Of this I have already treated. We cannot take a distinction which contrasts Creator and creature in terms of Father and Son, and then apply it to relations within the Godhead. While it is *essential* for Christian faith that we understand love in its deepest dimension in terms of the relation of Jesus to his heavenly Father, it spells only *confusion* for Christian faith to try to use the same symbols in reference to distinctions within the Godhead.

THE INTELLECTUAL CATEGORIES

Before passing to consider how it can best be expressed that God is love, I wish to digress for a moment to ask what validity attaches to use of the intellectual categories when we speak about God. We recognize that God made man in his image. The question is: where shall we find that image? Does it lie in man's self-awareness and rational nature? Since this is man's highest part, since in this he is distinguished from the animals, is this not the most fitting way to draw analogies with God? While we may recognize that intellect itself is an abstraction from man's total being, it is evident that any thinking about God and his image in us, involves some abstraction. Man is a creature, mortal and sinful; and none of this can apply to God. We have to abstract these features of man's nature from his existence as we know him, when we seek to find the resemblance between man and God. Yet while this is true, it may surely be questioned whether the most radical kind of abstraction, whereby only man's intellect is left, is the most fruitful way of discovering the image of God in him. For one thing, there is an infinite distinction between Creator and created, so that man's intellect is, in a sense, no nearer God than is his body. To speak of the "hand" of God or his right arm, is really no more misleading than to speak of God's mind or thought. All man's nature is creaturely, and as such infinitely removed from God's nature. Yet there *is* a similarity, and man's capacity for relations with God involves affirming this.

The issue is a very difficult one, and one that cannot be fully considered here. It may however, be helpful to observe that man has the capacity to be *like* God in many of his aspects. There are godlike qualities of love, mercy, and justice, which he is called to imitate in his heavenly Father. There is his capacity for creativity, whereby he is like God. There is, of course, his self-awareness, whereby he is a responsible person standing over against God and knowing him and seeking to do his will. We ought not then to abstract the intellect only, in order to find the image. We should find it as far as possible in his total being; and while we recognize this as created, mortal, and sinful, these are the only elements we can abstract from him, and of which we can say: here he is definitely *unlike* God. But in having feelings and imagination, in having the capacity to love and come into relations, in possessing vital powers of body as well as of intellect, in all these he is a person, and is not a real person apart from these qualities; and in consequence, in all these he is in some way like God, whom he encounters as a Person. Abstracting the intellect alone as the "image," both stems from the Greek underestimation of the body, the imagination, and the emotional life, which are considered as involved in the evil of matter, and also leads to a consequent disregard of the body. The Christian doctrine of the resurrection of the body is aimed to affirm the goodness of God's creation in this regard. The body is not, in itself, evil; and man is not a noble and eternal intellect unhappily encased in the prison house of the body. Man is a total being—body, feeling, and intellect, forming an interdependent and united whole; and God is not necessarily better spoken of as the One who thinks, than as the One who acts by his right hand. In all ways the Creator is infinitely above the creature. But as a person, man confronts God and has discourse with him. Here is the image: as a self-aware being, body and soul, thinking, feeling, acting, responsible, and creative, man is like God. But in no one of these manifold elements of his nature can we find the image, as if some particular one were so superior to all others that it in some way came nearer to God and transcended man's creatureliness. It is as a total person that man somehow resembles his Creator, just as it is that as a created being he is totally unlike him.

GOD AS LOVING HIMSELF

In the light of this let us now examine the two ways in which God has been thought of as the One who loves, and is not dependent merely upon his creation to express this. Somehow we must think of the Godhead as itself involved in the relations of love.

The first way in which this has been done is to think of God as a single person who loves himself. Once this symbol has been dissolved from its unhappy marriage with the problem of the Absolute, we can examine it with more freedom and on its own merits. There is patent religious value in such a way of thinking. It points us to the right kind of self-love; it reminds us that God is one, and deals with us as Person confronting person; it awakens us to the picture of God dynamically acting with singleness of will and purpose. Moreover, as Philo long ago contended, the symbol of God as one Person shows something of the distance between Creator and creature. When God created man he said, "It is not good that the man should be alone" (Gen. 2:18). For this reason he created Eve to be Adam's helpmate. Philo exegetes this to mean, "It is good that the Alone should be alone; for God, being one, is alone and unique, and like God there is nothing" (*Leg. All.* 2.1.1). But it was not good for man to be alone. He is unlike God, and, as such, dwells in society and realizes his nature by his relations with his fellows. Here his contrast with his Creator is made clear. The unity of God stands over against the diversity of man.

THE SOCIAL TRINITY

While, however, these values are to be seen in the symbol of God as loving himself, they need to be counterbalanced by another symbol—that of the Godhead in which there is more than one person. The picture of God as loving himself is open to two misrepresentations. His unity may be so conceived that the possibility of his coming into relations is endangered; he becomes the Absolute, and the unfortunate wedding of the symbol with the old paradox from which we have tried to separate it, is re-established. Or again, the unity of God comes to symbolize the loneliness of God, and the concept of love with which we started is endangered. To the Christian imagination loneliness is far from an appealing symbol. Love, as we know it, not only means the right kind of self-love, but also finds its expression and fulfillment in the mutual relations between living persons. Hence, while the picture of God as the one who loves himself, is important and necessary for the reasons we have given, it is insufficient. We reach another paradox—that God must be thought of *both* as the one who loves himself, *and* as a society in which persons enjoy the mutuality of love. To sacrifice either of these apparently contradictory symbols, is to sacrifice something essential that we must say; and to try to compose the paradox, is to introduce all sorts of confusions. Either the unity is swallowed up in the diversity, or the diversity is overcome by the unity.

The long struggle to find a fitting way to bring together these two symbols, both necessary as they are, has issued in nothing but futility. It has been argued: Is God a single center of self-consciousness, or is he three such centers? If he is the first, the full mutuality of love is insufficiently expressed; if he is the second, we have some kind of tritheism. There is ultimately no way in which we can solve this problem. Every solution hides within it the very paradox with which we begin. God is both the One and yet, in some sense, he must be thought of as a society. We cannot do justice to both necessary ideas if we try to find a way of bringing them into closer relation. We end up with arbitrary conceptions, which, however subtle they may be, cannot really overcome the essential paradox.

One of the first theologians to espouse the social doctrine of the Trinity was Richard St. Victor (*De Trin.* 3). He introduced the analogy of three persons who mutually love each other, on the ground that God's infinite goodness must be infinitely communicated, and this can only be done by three persons who stand in such relations with each other. To this Aquinas made his famous objection (*S.T.* 1. 31. 1 ad 2). He argued that *our* social communication of goodness rests on our "need to share some other's good in order to have the goodness of complete happiness." This, however, cannot be said of God, since he already *has* perfect happiness. For Aquinas, love is thus really a defect. We share in the goodness of others in order that we may acquire more goodness and be happier. This idea of love, of course, goes back to Plato. Love is striving, and always involves deficiency. The final contemplation of essential beauty is, for Plato, the cessation of the soul's dealings in love. For love is begotten of poverty and resource, and the self-sufficiency of contemplation involves neither love nor creativity (Symposium 208 ff.). But this is a most unsatisfactory conception. Sharing goodness is not aimed to *get* someone else's goodness or to fill up another's deficiency, but goodness itself lies in self-giving. It is this self-giving which is the essential element in the social Trinity, and we must have a way of expressing God's nature as eternally self-giving. We are thus driven to some symbol of God as society; but this has to be counterbalanced by the equally necessary symbol of God loving himself. The former alone would drive us into a plurality of gods; the latter, by itself, could never fully express what we mean when we speak of God as love.

The social doctrine of the Trinity has gained especial prominence in our day with its concern for social relations and with its understanding of love as personal fulfillment in society. Wilfred Richmond brought the doctrine to the fore in his *Essay on Personality,* and it has been given a vigorous expression in Leonard Hodgson's *The Doctrine of the Trinity.* In various ways these and other authors have tried to answer the obvious objection that it leads to tritheism. Richmond finds the unity of God in the fact that, while he is three personalities, "he is whole, complete in himself." Charles F. D'Arcy contends that God is "super-personal," and hence genuine personality can be predicated of each of the three persons in the Trinity.[4] John B. Champion in *Personality and the Trinity* lays greater stress on the unity and claims that there are in the Godhead three "Interpersonalities," which are "absolutely inseparable" from each other and which share an "interconsciousness or other-consciousness rather than self-consciousness."[5] Charles N. Bartlett, however, goes further in his *The Triune God,* and tries to find the unity in an underlying "subconscious" which all three share. He contends that there are "three active Self-consciousnesses freely exerted and yet absolutely controlled by the power of this underlying nature subconsciously and yet irrisistably dominant."[6]

It is, however, in Leonard Hodgson that the most striking attempt to solve the problem has been put forward. He contrasts the idea of mathematical unity with that of an "internally constitutive unity," to which the atom and the self are more analogous than the unity of arithmetic.[7] Mathematical unity means the "absence of multiplicity," whereas "approximation to the ideal of organic unity is measured by a scale of intensity of unifying power."[8] The unity is not heightened by *decreasing* the number and variety of the elements, but the reverse.[9] The three persons of the Trinity, thus, can constitute a real unity and yet not add up to the number one. The persons enjoying a mutual life of love are "intelligent, purposive centers of consciousness,"

[4] Art. "Trinity," in *Dictionary of Christ and the Gospels.*
[5] Pp. 66-7.
[6] P. 81.
[7] *The Doctrine of the Trinity,* pp. 105-107.
[8] *Ibid.,* p. 94.
[9] *Ibid.,* p. 95.

and by reason of their "intensive" unity constitute one God in this sense.

This is, to be sure, an attractive thesis, and it puts the matter with a clarity and forcefulness which are quite original. There are ways other than by mathematics of thinking about unity. But does Hodgson's "intensive" unity really overcome the problem of tritheism? The answer must surely be no. If there are three centers of consciousness in God, there are three gods; and no matter in what way we try to state their unity—be it one of purpose, or of an intensive relationship of love, or of an underlying essence—they are still three. Polytheism could claim some sort of "intensive" unity, so far as the gods shared the divine essence and dwelt in the heavens; and while it could be immediately objected that Hodgson's unity of the persons in the Christian Godhead is far *more* intensive, and the warfare and jealousy between the ancient gods have been overcome by a life of mutual self-giving, their individual character still remains. It is simply impossible to say that God is really one in some ultimate sense, and still retain the idea of discreet centers of consciousness, which stand over against each other. They qualify each other, as the elements of the atom or of the self qualify each other. As such they are limited, and the character of God is endangered. He ceases to be the one God who confronts us in an "I-Thou" relation, and who cannot be set over against another. He becomes involved in what is characteristic of the creature. Just to the extent that the unity which Hodgson conceives is really and finally intensive, the three centers of consciousness must merge themselves into one. Unless they do, along with the unity they display, they also display diversity and consequent limitation.

In fact, there is no way to overcome the paradox that we must think of God *both* as one and as a society. Logically he cannot be both; yet we must say both. Every attempt to find an underlying essence or unity in the three ends up either by really denying the three or by dividing the essence. The same would apply to the conception that three centers of consciousness have an underlying subconscious. For either there are really three subconsciousnessses to give a ground to each of the three consciousnesses, or the three consciousnesses are identical expressions of the one subconscious. There simply is no way in human thought to compose this paradox. Every solution, however ingenious, hides the paradox in one form or another. Is it not better to admit the paradox, to confess we have reached the limits of human thought, and to acknowledge that, to guard Christian truths, we must say self-contradictory things? There are basic reasons why we should symbolize God as one who loves himself; there are equally cogent reasons why we should say that God is in some sense like a society. Only in that way can we express fully what we mean when we declare God is love. And we must leave the matter there.

It may be well to add one final observation in connection with thinking of God as a person or as persons. It is this: these terms are only symbols. God is not a "self" or "selves" as *we* are. We cannot attribute to him the limitations of the creature; and part of the paradoxical nature of our necessary ways of thinking of him, derives from the fact that he is creator, we are creatures. The diversity we know within the self is no more to be attributed to him as he really is, than the diversity of discreet selves. All we can say is that in our encounter with him we meet him as a Person, and in our thinking about him we have to attribute to him the symbol both of one who loves himself and of a society of mutual love. But in neither case our language is literal. We say these things in order that the fullness of love may be ascribed to him, and that we may guard both his glory and his self-giving nature.

Before turning to consider the third term of the Trinity and the implicit problem of the "threeness" of God, we may digress for a moment to consider a central point which Hodgson makes in arriving at his view of the Trinity. He contends that his method is "the projection into eternity" of the essential relationship between Jesus and the Father. We have to assert that "eternally the Divine Life is a life of mutual self-giving to one another of Father and Son through the Spirit who is the *vinculum* or bond of love between them."[10] We have "to think away from the Son the accidents incidental to His revelation as incarnate, and to think away from the Spirit the accidents incidental to his revelation as inspiring incarnate beings."[11] It is by this process that Hodgson arrives at his Trinity of three self-conscious centers—Father, Son, and Spirit. As a method we can hardly object to the idea that the projection into eternity of the relation of Jesus to his heavenly Father, is a proper procedure whereby to understand God as self-giving. But the question is: has Hodgson carried his method through? Has he not left factors *incidental* to the incarnation in using the very terms Father and Son? While God's nature as love is disclosed in Jesus and his self-giving to the Father, that does not at all mean that the creaturely relation of the Son to his heavenly Father belongs in the Trinity. To express God as love we have to speak of his nature in some sense as resembling society. But to assume that

[10] *Ibid.*, p. 68.
[11] *Ibid.*, p. 84.

this can be put into categories of the Father and Son is quite unwarranted. Of this I have already treated, but it is mentioned here because it is so clearly apparent in Hodgson's argument. What he has, in fact, done is to apply to the Godhead, and to the necessary symbol of the Godhead as a society, factors that belong exclusively to the incarnation and the human Jesus. When we think of God as society, there is simply no reason for saying that the "persons" are Father and Son. That implies the one is in some way derived from the other, and we introduce a false solution to a quite different problem—that of God as absolute and as related. While it is true that an aspect of this issue is involved in our thinking of God as *one,* the central contrast of God as a person and as a society, is quite unrelated to the other paradox. It stems from different concerns and thus demands different symbols. In justice to Hodgson it must be remarked he wages warfare against the idea of the "monarchy" of the Father, as if he were really *more* God than the Son.[12] Yet he never satisfactorily establishes why the terms Father and Son are appropriate in the Trinity, save that they are derived from the revelation in Jesus.

[12] *Ibid.,* pp. 88 ff.

CHAPTER VI

THE SPIRIT AND THE TRINITY OF LOVE

THE THIRD TERM OF THE TRINITY IS THE SPIRIT. WE MUST NOW examine its meaning and place in the Godhead, and the consequent idea of "threeness" in speaking about God.

It has already been observed in former chapters that the Spirit in the biblical tradition is a term of wide meaning, referring to God as active in many ways in his creation. We have seen too that in the Trinity of mediation the place of the Spirit is largely, if not entirely, duplicated by that of the Logos, as far as his outward operations are concerned. The inspiration of the Scriptures can be associated with the one no less than with the other, just as the indwelling of God in the Christian convert can be understood as being "in Christ" or being "in the Spirit." Sometimes a clear identification of the terms emerges, as when Theophilus of Antioch speaks of the Word, "being God's Spirit" (Ad *Autol.* 3. 10), coming upon the prophets, and Justin sees the Spirit in the conception of Christ as none else than the Logos (I *Apol.* 33). Similarly the popular Christology reflected in Hermas treats the Spirit as the divine, creative Power which was united with the flesh in the incarnation (*Sim.* 5.6). Yet from New Testament times a distinction is made between the Word and the Spirit, trinitarian formulas appear,[1] and the explicit

[1] E.g., Theophilus, *op. cit.,* 2. 15.

identification of the terms is rare. Can we detect any effort clearly to differentiate them?

One of the first writers to suggest a distinct place for the Spirit in the Godhead is Athenagoras. He writes, "Since the Son is in the Father and the Father is in the Son by the unity and power of the Spirit, the Son of God is the mind and word of the Father" (*Plea,* 10). The Spirit is thus the uniting bond between Father and Son, the dynamic link by which their union is assured. The thought is not developed, but it is suggestive; and it is along these lines that Augustine worked out his notable pattern of the Trinity.

Before examining this, however, we may recall what has already been said regarding this idea of a link between the paradoxical modes of God's being as absolute and related. If "Father" means the former and "Son" the latter, as it does in so much early Christian thinking, then the attempt to establish a bond of unity between them is really to compose the original paradox. It all goes back to the effort to relate the Absolute to the world in terms of the fecundity of the former. In the ultimate analysis we become involved in all sorts of contradictions, and we may well ask: is it not better to *begin* with the essential contradiction and not try to overcome it? Every effort to compose the dilemma hides the paradox in one way or another. By the nature of the terms with which we start, we are doomed to failure in our effort to unify them. Hence the Spirit cannot be fruitfully conceived as the means by which God's absolute and related characters are composed.

The distinctive work of the Spirit in early Christianity was that of inspiring, hallowing, sanctifying. It is particularly in relation to the inspiration of the Scriptures that the Spirit is mentioned (as he is in Philo). Furthermore, as we have already seen, the ecstatic nature of early Christianity was viewed as the outpouring of the Spirit at the end of the days. Consequently the Spirit was more and more conceived as the internal work of God within the human heart. Sometimes, as in Montanism, this is associated with ecstasy; but usually the Spirit is conceived from a more distinctly ethical point of view. It is the principle of sainthood. Thus Origen can write that the Father is the source of existence; and that from the Son comes the natural gift of reason, from the Spirit the grace of *holiness* (*De Princ.* 1. 3. 8). Only in the saints does the Spirit dwell (*ibid.* 1. 3. 5), by which he means only the Christian convert possesses the Spirit.[2]

From this there develops the characteristic idea that the Spirit is the principle by which man is united to God. "Who will unite you to God," writes Athanasius in the controversy on the divinity of the Spirit, "if you have not the Spirit of God, but the spirit which belongs to creation?" (Ep. to Serapion, 1. 29). By participating in the Spirit we share in the divine nature and have communion with God (1. 24). The Spirit is thus that divine bond of unity, by which man is made capable of a renewed nature and of fellowship with God.

In a not dissimilar way, the Spirit plays his role in reference to hallowed *things*. By the Spirit the consecrated bread and wine acquire their divine quality in the Eucharist. They are sanctified, and become the body and blood of Christ. For this reason the Eastern church has laid such emphasis upon the epiklesis (or prayer of the Spirit's descent) in the liturgy. The Spirit is, to

[2] See Additional Note on Reason and Spirit, p. 115.

use the term in the creed of Gregory Thaumaturgus, "the provider of hallowing."

It was not, however, until Augustine that this conception of the Spirit, as the bond of union, was fully developed. In him the Spirit finds his place in the Godhead as the principle of unity. The Holy Spirit is "a certain unutterable communion of the Father and the Son," and hence is called both "holy" and "Spirit." The terms, to be sure, are fittingly applied to *all* the persons of the Trinity. But they are peculiarly appropriate to the third term as signifying the whole character of the Godhead, which this uniting principle implies (De Trin. 5. 11. 12). It is, furthermore, in the context of God as love, that Augustine's thought is unfolded. Not to unite the absolute mode of God's being with that of his coming into relation, but to show that God's nature is love, Augustine works out his idea. The communion or unity or holiness which links Father to Son is properly called "love." "And herein may be seen that the persons in the Trinity are three and not more than three. One who loves him who is from himself; and one who loves him from whom he is; and love itself" (6. 5. 7). The Spirit, in Augustine, is the love which Father and Son mutually share and give to each other. There can be only three in the Trinity, since there are only Father and Son and their common relationship.

The question may at once be raised whether this third term can properly be personified. If it is a term of relationship, can it be called a "person" in any legitimate sense? This has always been a crucial issue in Christian thinking about the Spirit. Father and Son in Christian art are frequently personified, but not the Spirit. He is symbolized by the dove or the rays descending from the Father; but personal pictures of the Spirit have been comparatively rare and, indeed, have been finally condemned (e.g., by Benedict XIV in the 18th century). While there are a few instances in early iconography, especially under the symbol of the visit of the three angels to Abraham (e.g., in San Vitale, Ravenna, 6th century), and while such pictures became somewhat more general from the ninth century onward, they have not prevailed in the Christian imagination. The Spirit has more frequently been conceived as "it" rather than as "he." The Spirit has been thought of as an effluence from the Father, a power of inspiration or hallowing, rather than as a "person."

This has been partly due to Augustine's treatment of the subject. The uniting bond of love cannot be viewed as personal in the same way as the Lover and the Beloved. The two personal terms are united by a *relationship,* and this is not a third person, but their principle of union. If two people love each other, their mutual love is merely the means whereby they are made one.

The matter, however, is more complex than this, for in Augustine the term "person" does not, in any full sense, belong to the three in the Trinity, but to the Trinity itself. The persons are themselves *relations* (7. 6. 12), while it is God, the Trinity, who is fittingly called a Person, over against his creatures (7. 4. 8). Thus the problem for Augustine is not so much how the Spirit can properly be personalized, as how Father and Son are, in his scheme, persons in any real sense. "We say three persons," he writes in an oft-quoted passage, "not that we wish to say it, but that we may not be reduced to silence" (7. 6. 11). His thought moves in the realm where the initial analogy between man and God, is that of *one* person. He understands the image of God in man as the image of the *Trinity;* and he finds this in the individual human being, not in three men (7. 6. 12). In consequence, and because he is dominated by the Neoplatonic concern for the One, his analogies all revolve around an analysis of what is characteristic of a single person. The mind, the love of itself, its knowledge of itself; memory, understanding, will; sight, object seen, attention of the mind—these are for Augustine the hints of the Trinity which he finds in the creature (*De Trin.* 9 and 10). The question, thus, is *not* that the Spirit differs from Father and Son, in Augustine, in being rather impersonal; but that *all* members of Augustine's Trinity are internal relations within the one personal God.

We have already pursued sufficiently this issue of the social Trinity over against the trinity of God's self-consciousness, and come to the conclusion that there are values in *both* analogies and that a paradoxical symbolism is essential to guard the whole Christian truth. We must think of God as loving himself, and we must also think of him as in some sense a society. Where Augustine introduces a real confusion is in attributing to all three persons of his Trinity the capacity to love. Persons may love, but relations cannot. His terms are highly ambiguous. How can the Father love the Son, if the Father is not the whole Trinity —i.e., the one personal God reflecting upon himself—but only a relation within it? And how can the Son love, if the Son is only the Father's thought of himself? Or the Spirit, if he is only the uniting love? That is the real problem for Augustine. By personalizing the relations in his symbolism, he introduces untold confusion.

What then, are we to say about the Spirit in the Trinity? The issue has been sharply raised in modern theology by Karl Barth, who takes over much of Augustine's way of thinking, and it may be profitable to examine his position. It revolves around two central points. The first is the clear distinction which he makes in contrasting the work of the Spirit with that of the Son. The second is the way in which he relates this to the internal relations within the Godhead.

The Spirit, he says, is "the subjective side in the event of revelation"[3] The contrast is between God's revelation as it is objectively presented to us, and as it is subjectively apprehended. This apprehension is not the work of man, but of God. Man does not stand toward revelation as if he were a partner with God in appropriating it. Man's "presence at revelation cannot be the presence of a partner or opposite." This means

> that from his presence no claims or privileges can arise for him as against God, that it can only be a factual, inconceivable, miraculous presence, factual because God is there; as we already stated, not only objectively but also subjectively, not only from above but also from below, not only from without but also from within.[4]

"By the doctrine of the divinity and the independence of the Spirit's divine mode of existence man is as it were called in question within his own house" (p. 535).

Here, in radical fashion to be sure, Barth clarifies the work of the Spirit over against that of the Son. He sharpens the contrast in objective-subjective terms, and limits the Spirit's operations to only one aspect of them in the Scriptures. This, however, is in line with the patristic development, as we have seen, where the Spirit is especially associated with God's indwelling. The objective-subjective contrast came to the fore in the liberal theology,

[3] *The Doctrine of the Word of God,* I, 515.
[4] *Ibid.,* pp. 535-36.

and Barth has taken it over with a vengeance. Where the liberal theologians distinguished the work of the Spirit from that of the Son, as God's "self-imparting" over against his "self-revealing," [5] Barth follows suit, but deprives man of the freedom which the liberal theology granted him in the divine encounter. That question, however, is irrelevant to our present study. What I wish to emphasize here is the sharp object-subject contrast as Barth conceives it.

This, in turn, indicates the place of the Spirit in the Godhead. What he is and does in revelation, "He is antecedently in himself." [6] In the Spirit's work upon us, he "does nothing else temporally than what he does eternally in God." [7] And what is that? "He is the common factor, or better, he is the communion, He is the act of the 'communityness' of the Father and the Son. He is the act in which the Father is the Father of the Son or the Speaker of the Word, and the Son is the Son of the Father, the Word of the Speaker." [8] Or again, "He is thus that love with which God (loves Himself i.e. loves Himself in each case as Father and Son, and so) as Father loves the Son, and as Son loves the Father." [9] The Spirit is thus the bond of union between Father and Son, and fulfills in the Godhead that same kind of subjective uniting which he fulfills in the event of revelation, whereby he relates us to God.

Now two further points may be noted. In the first place Barth does not think of the persons of the Trinity as real persons in the modern sense. They are modes of God's being. The Spirit is *not*

[5] E.g., William A. Brown in *Outline in Christian Theology*, p. 156.
[6] *The Doctrine of the Word of God, op. cit.*, p. 533.
[7] P. 539.
[8] *Ibid.*, p. 537.
[9] *Ibid.*, p. 537.

"a third spiritual subject, a third I . . . alongside two others," Father and the Son, but "a third mode of existence of the one divine Subject or Lord."[10] Personality in our sense, being an "I," is to be attributed to the whole Trinity, not to the modes of God's being.[11] Here Barth puts in current terms the very heart of Augustine's view. But having done this, he continues to speak of the Father and the Son as "loving" each other. But if they too are only modes of God's being, how can they love each other? If the "I" belongs to the Trinity rather than to the modes,[12] how can we speak of their mutual relations of love? What meaning can attach to saying that God as veiled loves God as unveiled, and that there is a common love between them? Here the confusions of Augustine are repeated. Barth, to be sure, is somewhat more cautious than Augustine, in that he tries to say that it is not the modes as such that love each other, but God *in* the modes. God as Father loves himself as Son, and as Son he loves himself as Father, and presumably, as Father or Son he loves himself as "love," and so on. But this does not really overcome the difficulty. If God loves himself, he loves himself; and there is no need to introduce his veiled and unveiled states into the process. As we have seen earlier in dealing with this question, the symbolism of God as love is not intrinsically related to his paradoxical modes of being, as beyond and in relation to the world.

Another confusion in Barth may be mentioned in passing, though it is not necessary to pursue it. He treats the Spirit's operations under the Roman Catholic rule of the appropriations,[13]

[10] *Ibid.*, p. 537.
[11] *Ibid.*, pp. 402-3.
[12] *Ibid.*, p. 403.
[13] *Ibid.*, pp. 429, 542.

but he does not keep consistently to this. He can write that the Spirit "also co-operates in creation in His own way."[14] But this is to destroy the whole idea of the appropriations. If the Spirit does something "in his own way," co-operating in an action, the work of the Trinity is divided up into several parts. The Roman rule forbids *any* distinctions to be made in the external operations of the Trinity.

The real question which emerges from Barth's treatment is the validity of this object-subject distinction. As far as it concerns the Godhead, it may well be asked why there must be a third term to unite the two modes of God's being. Not only is the symbolism of love highly unsatisfactory in this connection, as I have already pointed out, but also it is futile to search for a term of union by which to relate these self-contradictory but necessary ways of thinking of God. God is veiled, and he is unveiled (to use Barth's terms); he is absolute, yet related. Beyond that we cannot say anything more. The reason Barth seeks a term of union is because he thinks of God's mode of being as veiled, as in some sense *prior* to his unveiling. Behind this lurks the old idea of bringing the Absolute into relation by its fecundity. Such metaphysical ideas Barth would doubtless vigorously disclaim. But they are implicit in the way he sets up the initial distinctions of the Trinity. God distinguishes himself from himself. First and foremost it is his nature to be God "hiddenly." God in "His nature cannot be unveiled to man."[15] But he *does* graciously reveal himself. He chooses to become manifest, "i.e. in the form of something He Himself is not, to be God a second time."[16] This

[14] *Ibid.*, p. 539.
[15] *Ibid.*, p. 362.
[16] *Ibid.*, p. 363.

puts in categories of revelation the old contrast so much belabored here. It is a paradox, an essential one; but no way of composing it is open to us. To introduce the ambiguous symbolism of Augustine at this point does not assist us. Rather it adds confusion to a dubious solution of the problem. For if God in his initial mode of being is absolutely hidden, his revealed mode of being can in no way be derived or deduced from this. To contend a relation between them can be established by the principle of love, is merely to read back the whole paradox into the first term of the dilemma. If it is because God, as hidden, *loves,* that he becomes revealed, then his hiddenness is no longer fully hiddenness. The principle of self-revealing, which love means, is already implicit in it. Thus the two modes of God's being, as Barth defines them, are immediately present in the first mode. Every attempt to solve this, or any other similar paradox, ends in failure. Either the paradox lurks unsolved somewhere in the supposed solution, or one of the two terms is compromised.

We turn now to examine the validity of the subject-object distinction as it touches the work of the Spirit. If we are going to make any coherent contrast between the operations of the Spirit and those of the Son, it must surely be this. Although the distinction is not entirely true to the Scriptures—since the symbolism there of the Divinity it still unclarified and in a fluid state—it is the most persuasive one; and there is much in the New Testament, as well as in the early Christian tradition, to support it. Moreover, it points to a most fundamental aspect of our experience. It is not by our own effort, by our wisdom and willingness, that we respond to God's revelation in Jesus Christ. We call Jesus "Lord" *in the Spirit* (I Cor. 12:3). Confronted with God's objective revelation, we are aware that our appropriation of it is the work of God himself. It is only as he enables us to transcend our limitations, that our eyes are opened and our hearts enabled to embrace his own gift. God's self-revealing is only completed in his self-imparting. Our response is *his* own response in us. While it may be argued that Barth somewhat overstates this truth, so that man's freedom is really denied, it is nonetheless true that he understands with great perception the importance of this cardinal aspect of the Christian gospel. Not by our own strength or by our own capacity can we grasp and be grasped by the divine reality of Jesus Christ, nor can we by any instance of God's revelation. The work is God's both outwardly and inwardly; and our encounter with God in terms of his Spirit within us is thoroughly personal. The Spirit is not a vague effluence or impersonal power, but God himself at work in us, witnessing, responding, interceding.

The question, however, is whether this leads us necessarily to say that the Spirit is an entity over against the Son, that God exists in a third mode of being as the self-imparter. Granted that the distinction is of crucial importance as *we* look at the matter—differentiating God's inward working from his objective presentation of himself in the revealing event—does this mean that the distinction is to be carried back to the Godhead? In order that it may find a proper metaphysical ground, must the distinction be so grounded in the Godhead?

It is here that an objection must be entered. The difference between God's self-imparting and his self-revealing is not a difference which leads us to distinguish two separate persons in the Trinity. The subject-object relation touches our apprehension of different ways in which God works; it does not necessitate our making a final distinction in the Godhead. Both are aspects of

God as he relates himself to us. He does this in many ways; and the difference between his inward and outward working is no greater than the difference between the manifold other ways in which he unveils himself—in creation, in the law, in the prophets, or in Jesus. "In many and various ways" (R.S.V.) has God spoken, as the author of the *Epistle to the Hebrews* says. We can distinguish these ways, but the distinctions do not lead back to distinctions in the Godhead. They are all aspects of God in his relations with us. We do not seek a separate person in the Godhead to account for each particular act of God's revelation—one for the burning bush, another for the Red Sea, another again for the inspiration of the Scriptures, and still another for the revelation in Jesus or in the Church. These are all aspects of one single divine reality—God in his relations with his world. They are modes of God's operations, distinguishable indeed, but not distinguishable *in principle.* The Spirit and the Word are two ways of saying the same thing—that over against God's transcendent mystery, he comes to us, revealing, inspiring and re-creating. It is the same Spirit by which he created, by which he led Israel on her spiritual journey, by which he finally declared himself in the life and deeds of Jesus, and by which he continues to work in the Church's history. He works inwardly and outwardly; he declares himself in the law and in the prophets and in the gospel; he unveils himself to some degree in creation. But in all these ways it is the one Spirit of God which is at work and whom we encounter as "person" over against us, both in our beholding and in our appropriating his revelation. The object-subject distinction is no deeper than other distinctions we make in speaking of God's manifold relations with his world.

The consequence of finding a different person in the Godhead to account for each distinct way in which God comes to us is to have a Trinity with an infinite number of terms. The variety of creation demands a variety in God's relationships with it, and the subject-object contrast is only one of these. Persons or modes of being in the Godhead can only be fittingly posited from the point of view of paradoxical or apparently self-contradictory ways in which we must affirm that God exists. The subject-object distinction does not belong to this category. It is only one among a great variety of aspects by which God comes into relationship. He who seizes and possesses man to grasp and be grasped by a revealing event, is the same One who seizes and possesses the man in whom the revealing event occurs, or seizes and possesses some aspect of nature to declare himself in some way. Distinctions we must affirm in the Godhead, but they are not distinctions about the different ways in which God relates himself to the world. The God of the Old Testament is not a distinct person of the Trinity, over against the God of the New Testament. No more is the God who works inwardly in us to be differentiated as a person of the Trinity, distinct from the God who presents himself to us outwardly.

The "threeness" of the Trinity is an arbitrary and unpersuasive doctrine. It has arisen partly because the New Testament presents us with three dominant symbols of God. But as we have seen, the symbolism there is still in a fluid state, and the work of the Son and of the Spirit tend to overlap. It has arisen, again, because of the desire to compose the essential paradox of God's absolute and related character and to find a term of union between these. Of the fruitlessness of that quest enough has already been said. It has arisen again, as a way of understanding God as love. But here too the third term is arbitrary. If, as we have seen, we picture God as loving himself, the threefoldness of this process does not resolve itself into three persons. There is Lover and Beloved; but their term of union, their mutual love, is not a person. Moreover, this threefold analysis of the process of self-love is itself open to grave question. God does not love his thought of himself but *himself,* nor can his thought of himself love him in return. Personalizing inner relations leads to all sorts of confusion. Furthermore, if we analyze the process of self-love, we by no means are confined to three terms. Even if inner relations could be satisfactorily regarded as a basis upon which to build analogies with the Godhead, we could never stop with three. Augustine's psychological analogies, like those in Aquinas who follows him, are arbitrary in the highest degree so far as their threefold nature goes. If we speak of memory, will, and intellect, where is imagination? If we speak of conscious relations, where is the unconscious ground? The fact of the matter is, an analysis of inner relations can be posed in an indefinite number of terms. There is no necessity about the number three.

The same must be said when we consider how God can in some sense be a society. With the importance of the social analogy to counterbalance the picture of God as loving himself, I have already dealt. Here I shall note only that such a society does not imply the number three. It involves only a second term, as far as there are Lover and Beloved; it does not necessitate a third. The mutual love is implicit in the two. Once, however, the magic spell of unity is broken, we are inevitably driven to an indefinite number. If society is our analogy with the Godhead, then the more members there are, the more love abounds. Hodgson is in one sense right when he observes that "intensive unity" (as he calls it) is heightened rather than lessened by increasing the number and variety of the elements.[17] The logic of this should perhaps have driven Hodgson to posit an *infinite* number of persons in the Trinity. To stop at three is to have a *less* intensive unity than there might be. However this may be, certain it is that the social analogy with the Trinity involves at least two terms and at most an indefinite number. But three terms is an arbitrary way of conceiving the matter.

That these terms, furthermore, can fittingly be called "Father" and "Son" raises many issues on which I have already dwelt. The primary difficulty of such language is the assumption of the derivation of one term from the other. This, as I have tried to show, is an illicit assumption when we are speaking of the Godhead. Furthermore, we cannot attribute to relations within the divinity, terms which really have their origin in a relationship of the Creator with his creature. Such terms properly belong to the incarnate state and cannot be driven back to the Godhead. While it is *fundamental* for Christian faith to assert that we come to understand the full meaning of love when we consider the mutual self-giving between Jesus and his heavenly Father, it only leads us into endless difficulty to read back these terms of the incarnate life into the Godhead. Whether we think of God as loving himself or as in some sense analogous with a society, it is not in any terms of Father and Son that we can fittingly express this. As a theological statement, we must be content with saying only that God both loves himself *and* in some way resembles a society.

The conclusion that the symbols Spirit and Son are really identical and are two ways of speaking of God's relations with us—

[17] *Op. cit.*, p. 95.

ways to be distinguished, to be sure, as *we* encounter God within us and in his disclosure in revelation, but not to be distinguished as persons within the Godhead—necessarily leads to a final point. The doctrines of the *procession* of the Spirit (in contrast to the *begetting* of the Son), and of the *filioque* (i.e., whether the Spirit proceeds *from* or only *through* the Son), can no longer be regarded as legitimate theological issues. They rest upon a type of distinction that I have tried to show is gratuitous and arbitrary, and in consequence they wrestle with issues which are not real issues. They derive from a false posing of the initial distinctions in the Godhead. While they have rent the Church and engendered much subtle argument, they go back to unsatisfactory structures of thought. They have meaning only when the Spirit is viewed as a divine entity or relation over against the Son. Hence it is not needful to pursue them here. Almost at the end of his great work on the Trinity, Augustine finds himself still worried in his effort to distinguish the begetting of the Son from the procession of the Spirit. His solution is to contrast the will or love which combines the memory with its begotten word, and the process whereby the word is made the offspring of its parent (15. 27. 50). But if, as I have tried to show, this whole way of drawing analogies with the Godhead is open to question, the distinction is not helpful.

The same is to be said of the filioque. The Western position, whereby the Spirit is viewed as proceeding from the Father *and* the Son, has behind it the desire to stress the *equality* of the Son with the Father. The doctrine emerged in a context of opposition to Arianism. The Eastern objection to this (and especially to the insertion of the phrase into the Creed) is based upon the contention that such modes of expression posit two principles of causality in the divine. These refinements of theological debate, however, cannot but be regarded as unnecessary, once the identity of what we mean by "Spirit" and "Son" in reference to the Godhead is acknowledged.

ADDITIONAL NOTE ON REASON AND SPIRIT

It has sometimes been contended, in the light of such a statement of Origen (see p. 100), that the controversy in the early Church over the divinity of the Holy Spirit concerned the distinction between man's rationality and the divine gift of "spirituality," which was superior to this. The refusal, for instance, of the followers of Eusebius of Caesarea to admit the divinity of the Spirit, meant their desire to conform Christianity to culture and to interpret the work of the Son as the Logos, solely in rational terms. Thus the Church was not distinct from the Christian empire as the realm of the divine Spirit, but rather an aspect of that empire exemplifying in a special way the triumph of the principle of reason. While there is an element of truth in this, four basic factors must be borne in mind.

1. In the earlier period in which the *identity* of the Spirit with the Son was occasionally overtly expressed and generally in principle implied, the Son as the Logos did *not* mean that the Son was "Reason" in our modern sense. The word "logos" was, of course, ambiguous, standing at once for "reason" and "word." Under the term, however, there was summed up a great variety of religious and ethical ideas. The Logos was primarily God's *Word*—his declaration of salvation in Jesus Christ. This, indeed, *did* have overtones from the Hellenic tradition of rationality, of right thinking, insofar as the pious heathen were viewed as forerunners of the gospel (cf. Justin, 1 *Apol.* 46). But what de-

termined the content of Logos was the message and life of Jesus, not man's general notions of what was rational or right. To live "according to *logos*" meant to live the "reasonable" Christian life as the gospel defined it. As far as Spirit and Word were identical in principle, they referred to God's relations with his world in a variety of ways. He declared himself in the human conscience, in the law, in the prophets, in Jesus, and in the internal witness of the Church and the Christian heart.

2. In the later, fourth-century period, in which the Spirit's divinity was called in question, the issue was *not* posed from the possibility of the identification of the Son and the Spirit. Their distinction was affirmed by all parties on the basis of scriptural texts where they were clearly differentiated.

3. The Arian parties disputed the full deity of the Son. Hence for them the Spirit was an even more inferior "power" of God than the Son, since the former stood third in the descending chain of being, and was excluded from the creative function of the Logos. It can hardly be denied that the conformity of the Church to culture was implicit in the Arian position. But this was *not* because they denied the deity of the Spirit, *but* because they questioned the deity of the Son. This they did on a highly rational basis, separating God from the world in such a way that divinity does not enter human history. Salvation was endangered, and the Church was no longer the fellowship in which God himself was at work. In consequence the Church was in danger of being swallowed up in culture. Its distinctive nature and mission were called in question.

4. The denial of the divinity of the Spirit by those who *accepted* the deity of the Son, is a confused and difficult issue. We may perhaps distinguish those who questioned the Spirit's

divinity because the Godhead of the Spirit was not totally clear in the Scriptures, from those who did so to avoid accepting a principle superior to that of rationality. The latter might well apply to the party of Eusebius of Caesarea.[18] The former would be represented by the Tropici against whom Athanasius directed his letters to Serapion.

[18] See G. Kretschmar, *Studien zur Frühchristlichen Trinitätstheologie,* 1956, pp. 1-15.

CHAPTER VII

THE TRINITY OF REVELATION

PRACTICAL CHRISTIANITY THROUGH THE CENTURIES HAS TENDED TO avoid those speculations of trinitarian thinking which have so far engaged us. Popular faith is not concerned with relating the Absolute to the Relative, or with wondering how the diverse modes of God's being can be resolved into an ultimate unity. The practical Christian finds himself confronted with different ways in which God has revealed himself, and is content to think of the Trinity from this point of view. God, for him, is one Person, whom he encounters in various experiences. The one God makes himself manifest in a diversity of ways. He has, as it were, different "names"; but behind these there lies the one personal God to whom his faith is directed and whose judgment and love he apprehends in Jesus Christ. The metaphysical ground of these names—the way in which they may imply different modes of being in the Godhead—is not his concern. Rather his view of the Trinity springs from the demands of practical piety. The man of faith will worship the one God as he manifests himself in experience.

This attitude toward the Trinity is connected especially with the name of Sabellius. It has, however, had a number of variant forms in Christian history, and it is best approached from the Apostles' Creed. For the average man the declarations of this creed have always seemed more intelligible than those of the so-called Nicene Creed, which incorporated themes from the metaphysical debates of the fourth century. The Apostles' Creed, on the other hand, makes clear and succinct affirmations, which appear to avoid subtle speculation.

In the precise form in which it is familiar to us, this creed belongs to the eighth century. But already by A.D. 400 it had acquired more or less its present shape; and, in turn, this goes back to the baptismal creed of the Roman church. Originally, it was composed of three short questions put to the candidate, and to which he gave his assent as he was thrice dipped in the water. He was asked, "Do you believe in God the Father Almighty?" To this the candidate responded, "I believe." There followed the question, "Do you believe in Christ Jesus, the Son of God, who was born of the Holy Spirit and the Virgin Mary [and so on, reciting the crucial events of the passion and resurrection]?" Finally, "Do you believe in the Holy Spirit, in the holy Church, and the resurrection of the flesh?" (Hipp. *Apost. Trad.* 21.12 ff.).

This triple creed thus affirmed God the Father as creator, God the Son as redeemer, and God the Holy Spirit as sanctifier in the church. The Trinity was one of God's revelation. He made himself known in three distinct ways and in the context of three experiences; i.e., as creator, redeemer and sanctifier. Later on, various additions were made to this creed, to bring out more fully the sense of these basic affirmations. One such clarification was the addition of the words, "Maker of heaven and earth," to qualify, "God, the Father Almighty." The phrase appears first in the sixth century, and was doubtless inserted because the term Father was increasingly being limited to refer to the unique relation of the first person of the Trinity to the second. Thus its original connotation of "Creator," derived from the Hebrew tradition and current in the primitive Christian usage where it meant "Father and Creator of the universe" (I Clem. 19 and 35), was becoming obscured. Similarly, the term Almighty was, under the influence of Greek thought, becoming understood as "able to do anything," instead of as "all-ruling"; and the words "Maker of heaven and earth" helped to restore its original sense.

It was in the context of this practical faith which encountered God in his creation, in his redeeming work in Jesus, and in his self-imparting in the Spirit, that the doctrine later known as Sabellianism developed. This is not for a moment to suggest that the Roman creed was Sabellian in intent. Quite the contrary; it arose in thoroughly orthodox circles, though it could, indeed, be recited by Christians who held varying viewpoints on the Trinity. The important thing, however, is that it reflects the type of popular piety which proved a fertile soil for the development of Sabellius' ideas. What were these ideas?

Our sources for understanding precisely what Sabellius taught in the early third century are scanty and, on one crucial point, contradictory. Perhaps the most reliable account is in Theodoret (*Haer. Fab.* 2.9). "Sabellius said that Father, Son and Spirit were one *hypostasis,* one person (*prosopon*) under three names, and he describes the same one now as Father, now as Son, now as Holy Spirit. He says that in the Old Testament he gave laws as Father, was incarnate in the New Testament as the Son, and visited the apostles as the Holy Spirit." This statement is cogent and clear. Sabellius taught that God was *one* Person, and had three names which referred to his revelation first as Lawgiver, then as Redeemer, finally as Sanctifier. Another, but less reliable, account attributes to Sabellius the teaching that God was three persons, but these persons were only "faces," or "masks" or "roles" which the one God assumed according to circumstances (Basil, Ep. 210.3, 5; 214.3; 236.6). From this has arisen the popular misconception that he used the term "person" (or *prosopon*) in this qualified sense, and that hence the Greek fathers later avoided the word. This, however, is not so. While the fathers preferred the more technical term "hypostasis," they *did* use the word "prosopon." Basil is perhaps making inferences from Sabellius' teaching, or else he is referring to views of his later followers.

The important thing, however, is that Sabellius devised a theory adapted to the unreflective nature of popular piety. God is one Person, but makes himself evident under different names in different contexts and experiences. But it is all one God. Father and Son are not two different beings, but one and the same. When we think of him as giving laws in the Old Testament, we call him "Father." When we think of him manifest in Jesus, we say "Son." But these are only names. Just as a man may be known as "President" or "General" or "John" in his different relations and according to circumstance, but is still the same person, so it is with God. The names declare how he is related to us at different times and in various ways. But it is the same, one person who is made manifest.

Sabellius' view was not original. He had learned it, directly or indirectly, from others, such as Noetus and a shadowy figure we hear of, called Cleomenes. But he undoubtedly refined what had at first been a very naïve conception. To identify God and Jesus spoke to the demands of popular piety. Jesus *was* the Saviour God; no distinction could be made between him and the Father. He was God made manifest in the flesh. "Why, what harm have I done?" Noetus replied to his antagonists who finally excommunicated him. "I believe in one God" (Hipp. *Con. Noet.*

1). Or again, "What harm am I doing in glorifying Christ?" (Epiph. Pan. 57). The refinement which Sabellius introduced was the way in which he thought of the first name of God. He applied this not to God as creator in general, but to God as the lawgiver of the Old Testament. The names of God were very distinctly, for him, names which referred to God's *particular* acts of revelation. It was not to defend "natural" revelation—the idea that God is in some way made manifest in all creation—but to denote God's *specific* acts of self-revealing, that the names were used. The deeply religious concern of Sabellius is here very apparent.

Against the views of Sabellius and those further refined by his successors, which we need not elaborate here, one fundamental change was made—that of Patripassianism. His theory involved the assumption that God the Father himself suffered. It conditioned the unconditioned; it robbed God of his final transcendence. He who is pure light and joy and impassible, was involved in the ignominy of pain and suffering. I have already treated this problem in a previous chapter, and need not repeat here the conclusions. Two points, however, must be mentioned. Sabellius' teaching does in the final analysis fail to make an adequate distinction in the Godhead. It does not grasp the necessity of speaking of paradoxical modes of being in God. Yet the charge brought against him does, itself, often fail to apprehend fully the truth which Sabellius was trying to express. God *does* become involved in suffering for the world's redemption. That is the very heart of the Christian gospel. But the attempt to solve this by saying that the Son is somewhat *nearer* the possibility of suffering than the Father, because he is begotten of the Father is misleading in the extreme. It suggests that he is not quite

God, and so can appropriate the sufferings of the humanity, in a way the Father does not and cannot. Such a way of putting it fails to do full justice to the Christian mystery, which can only be expressed paradoxically: God is perfect joy, and yet he enters into suffering to redeem.

One other point may be noted. It is often contended that the weakness of Sabellius' position lay in the assumption that God himself "as a whole, so to speak, comes forth in revelation," so that there "nothing is left behind."[1] So far as this touches the previous point, it is true. But Sabellius would doubtless have replied that something of the *same charge* could be brought against the Logos Christology. Even the Logos, as incarnate, does not "as a whole" come forth in revelation. There is always something "left behind." He is still agent of creation, still impassible in his divine nature. No; that is not the way to express it. What we have to say is that God *both* is joy and appropriates suffering. There is a final paradox in his being—an antinomy—which no terms of begetting can overcome.

To the question whether it is possible to devise a Trinity from the point of view of God's modes or acts of revelation, the answer must be negative on two scores. Such a Trinity fails to make essential distinctions in the Godhead, to preserve at once God's absolute and related character. But it fails in more than this. It also sets up an arbitrary threefoldness in understanding God's revelation. The threefold category may be useful, but it is not essential. We know God in a great variety of ways, and the manner in which we schematize these has no necessary element in it. God unveils himself to us in some manner in his creation,

[1] J. F. Bethune-Baker, *Introduction to the Early History of Christian Doctrine,* p. 106.

and again in the Old Testament law. In yet different ways he is manifest in the Old Testament prophets, in the revelation in Jesus, in the work and life of the Church, and in the internal witness by which we respond to his manifold revelations. All these modes of God's self-unveiling are different. Each has a specific character and quality of its own. Indeed, in every event of his unveiling and in every response to it there is a unique and unrepeatable element. We may classify these in various ways for our convenience. Some resemble others more closely. Others, in turn, seem radically to differ from yet others. But the variety of God's operations is such that they can never constitute a genuine Trinity.

The views of Sabellius, in one form or another, have reappeared in the course of the church's history. Within modern times, they have been championed by Friedrich Schleiermacher, who in a famous essay sought to rehabilitate that ancient writer and to reinterpret him. From Schleiermacher a view of the Trinity founded on Christian experience and expressing the threefold nature of God's revelation, became current in the Liberal Theology. The essence of Schleiermacher's position was succinctly put by him thus: "In governing the world in all its various operations on finite beings, the Godhead is Father. As redeeming, by special operations in the person of Christ and through him, it is Son. As sanctifying, and in all its operations on the community of believers and as a Unity in the same, the Godhead is Spirit." [2] The persons of the Godhead are thus names we give to his different operations as we experience them. The presupposition of Schleiermacher is that God is the Monad: "God

[2] Translation of his essay by Moses Stuart in the *Biblical Repository,* 1835, VI, 70.

is the unconditioned and absolutely simple."[3] No distinctions or differentiations can be made in his being. "The trinity, therefore, is God revealed; and each member of the same is a particular mode of this revelation."[4]

The translator of Schleiermacher's essay, however, goes beyond the great German theologian in showing that the Trinity of revelation can be stated in a more satisfactory way. We can overcome some of the objections raised against Sabellius if we do not regard these names purely as transitory and successive phases of revelation (as they appear to be in Sabellius), but ground them *ontologically* in the Godhead. Stuart writes: "There was in the Godhead, antecedent to creation and redemption, something which was the foundation of all the developments made in the same."[5] What these distinctions actually *are* in the Godhead, we can, indeed, never fully know. That is something not "given to created intelligences" to describe.[6] But we are not forced to hold the simplicity of the divine essence in the stark way that Schleiermacher does. The threefold revelation bespeaks eternal distinctions, though we can never penetrate them. Such a position does not, however, really answer the two deepest objections to be brought against Sabellius. Even given the fact that the threefold mode of God's self-revealing has an eternal ground in God, this does not clarify the fundamental paradox of God's absolute and related character, nor does it cogently show the necessary threeness of these distinctions. It is not in the manner or manners in which God is revealed that the primary problem lies. Rather is it to be seen in the fact that beside his revealed and related nature,

[3] *The Christian Faith,* par. 172.1.
[4] *Biblical Repository,* VI, 61.
[5] *Ibid.,* p. 95.
[6] *Ibid.,* p. 96.

there stands his hiddenness and beyondness. It is the self-contradictory nature of this contrast that forms the starting point for distinctions in the Godhead. Of the other point, concerning the arbitrary threeness of this view of revelation, I have already sufficiently spoken.

The matter is finally summed up by William Adams Brown, the "dean" of American Liberal Theology, in his *Christian Theology in Outline.*[7] There he interprets the Trinity in terms of the necessary ways we have of thinking about God. We "may think of him as the Absolute, the ultimate source of all being and life, himself surpassing man's ability perfectly to comprehend" him. Again, we "may think of him as the self-revealing one, known to men through his revelation in nature, in history and, above all, in Christ." Finally, we "may think of him as the self-imparting one, known through direct experience in the consciousness of man as the source of the spiritual life." This is the experiential Trinity; but it has passed beyond the terms of Schleiermacher. God's absolute character becomes the first term, and then his revealed and self-imparting nature. This surely is a step in the right direction. But there still is assumed that the Absolute is "the ultimate source of all being"—an idea which we have seen in Plato, and which involves an inner contradiction. The paradoxical nature of God as absolute and as related is not fully grasped. Furthermore, the distinction between God as revealed and as self-imparted is used to characterize the second and third persons. Of the difficulty with this I have already treated in the previous chapter. From it we cannot derive a genuine Trinity.

[7] P. 156.

We conclude, then, that a Trinity of revelation is unsatisfactory. As proposed by Sabellius and Schleiermacher, it speaks of only one term in the paradox of God's being—his relationship with us. And so far as it expresses and analyzes this, it arrives at an arbitrary threeness.

One further attempt to understand the Trinity in terms of God's revealing activity must now engage us. It is to be sharply distinguished from Sabellianism, and has been put forward by Claude Welch in his instructive and often penetrating survey of modern trinitarian doctrines, *In This Name*. He tries to establish a Trinity on the basis of the necessary threefold *structure* in each revealing act of God.

Welch criticizes the revised Sabellian Trinity, which attempts to ground the threefold *content* of the divine activity (i.e., God as creator, redeemer, and sanctifier) in the being of God, for the reason that this involves "an intolerable division" in the ethical nature of God. It violates the rule whereby we have to view God's external operations as indivisible.[8] Otherwise we divide the unity of God's essence. This criticism is perhaps not so serious as others to be brought against the doctrine—others which have already been examined. All distinctions we are forced to make in the Godhead do in effect divide the essence, and there is no way of overcoming this. We are led to state paradoxes—to affirm the simplicity of the divine essence and the unity of God, while at the same time acknowledging necessary distinctions. Human thought is confronted with antinomies, which it cannot surmount. However this may be, having found monarchian views unacceptable, Welch attempts a reconstruction of trinitarian doctrine on the basis of the structure of revelation.

[8] Pp. 220-1.

It is, he claims, the "*mode* or *form* of revelation," which is the starting point for a doctrine of the Trinity. There is a

> distinction in the act of revelation or redemption between *him* who stands above and apart as the one to whom Jesus points and to whom everything is referred, who is the presupposition of the work in Christ; *him* who confronts man in Jesus Christ as the objective content of revelation; and *him* who seizes and possesses man so that he is able to receive and participate in revelation, new life, salvation. This distinction the New Testament indicates by the words Father, Son and Holy Spirit.[9]

From these contrasts Welch establishes his Trinity, and he relates them intrinsically to those distinctions in God whereby he is known as love. His "perfect and infinite personality" is characterized by an inner relatedness and mutuality, which are expressed by the community between Father and Son through the Spirit.[10]

There are three implications of this point of view, which we must examine. Is the analysis of the structure of revelation adequate? Are the distinctions fittingly to be referred to as Father, Son, and Spirit? Do these distinctions bear a necessary and intrinsic relation to the mutuality and self-giving to be acknowledged in the personality of God?

First, with regard to the adequacy of the analysis: are there really three "*him's*" as Welch defines them? On the surface it might seem to be so. In the person of Jesus Christ, manifest in history as a real human being, we encounter one "him." He in turn points us to his Father—a second "him." Furthermore, we

[9] *Ibid.*, p. 222.
[10] *Ibid.*, pp. 287 ff.

apprehend God's revealing act in Jesus as we experience the Spirit—a third "him"—speaking in our hearts. Is this not, however, to introduce a number of confusions, when we try to apply these "him's" to the Godhead, as if they were really three?

To what, for instance, does the "him" precisely refer, when we consider God's revelation in Jesus? If we are speaking of the *man,* Jesus of Nazareth, the "him" implies the accidents of the incarnation, which we certainly cannot read back into the Godhead. But insofar as the "him" refers to God himself, who is made manifest in the historical life, we are speaking of elements in the term Father, to the extent that this includes that aspect, or mode of being, of God whereby he comes into relation with us. Of the ambiguity of this term we have dealt in former chapters, and the way in which Welch defines the three "him's" does nothing to clarify this ambiguity. If "Father" means the God who is "above and beyond," in contrast to him who is unveiled and encountered, then we certainly have two "him's"—two paradoxical modes of God's being. But they are not to be defined by contrasting the Father with Jesus. They are to be defined in terms of God's absolute beyondness and his unveiling. Since, furthermore, as even Welch admits,[11] every revealing act involves these "him's," our statement must avoid speaking of only the revelation in Jesus. It must be broad enough to cover every event of God's unveiling.

When we come next to the third "him," as Welch defines it, we meet an issue which has already been sufficiently treated. The one who seizes and possesses us to respond to the act of revelation, is precisely the *same* one who is present in the objective act.

[11] *Ibid.,* p. 223.

There are not two "him's" to be discriminated. There is God in his relations with us. These relations differ, to be sure. We can contrast God as subjectively apprehended and as objectively manifest. But this difference is no greater than other differences we are forced to make in discerning God's manifold operations. In every revealing event there is a unique element, and surely we are not going to assume a different "him" in each instance—one for the Law, one for the prophets, one for the gospel, one for subjective apprehension, and so on. There is no third term necessary. All that is required is that we contrast God in his absolute transcendence, with God in his manifold unveiling and relations with his creatures. The analysis of the three "him's," therefore, as Welch proposes them, is inadequate. It is ambiguous and involves an arbitrary "threeness."

To our second question whether the distinctions in the Godhead are fittingly referred to as Father, Son, and Spirit, we may observe only this. Certainly the New Testament presents us with these three dominant symbols, and they point to vital aspects of the Christian gospel; but this does not mean that they define three different persons of the Godhead. The New Testament symbolism, as we have seen, is still in a fluid state. The names of God tend to overlap, and for clarity's sake we have to use more precise language as we try to grasp what lies behind them. In our final chapter we shall show what these terms may mean to us, but their ambiguity (especially that of the "Father") makes them inadequate as exact terms by which to denominate distinctions in the Godhead.

Turning to our third question, we find that the distinctions as Welch defines them do not bear an essential relation to God's being as love. The God who is made present in his revealing acts is not a person over against God in his transcendent glory, in such a way that they mutually love each other. Nor is God, imparting himself in the heart, someone or some "thing" or "relation,"[12] distinct from God as revealing himself in the objective act. As we have seen in a former chapter, the symbols by which we try to express God as love are not intrinsically connected with the way in which we speak of his absolute and related character. God's beyondness does not love his relatedness, any more than his wrath loves his love. Love is a term of union, and there is no way by which to unite this necessary paradox of God's being without compromising one or other of the truths we seek to affirm. The "relatedness or mutuality" which Welch applies to God as "perfect, self-sufficient personality," is not to be found in discriminating the Father who "stands above and apart," from the One whom we encounter in the act of revelation.[13] Paradoxical modes of God's being do not imply relations of love. We are mixing up two different questions, two different sets of symbols, by trying to explain God as love on the basis of distinctions in the structure of revelation.

Finally, as far as Welch tries to speak of the being of God as love, by avoiding the dangers of tritheism in the social Trinity, he defines the matter thus: "Perfect or infinite personality contains within itself the relatedness or mutuality which is external in the case of the finite person."[14] God, he claims, is not a self-sufficient personality by being a society of selves, since the addition of incomplete and dependent selves will never total an

[12] Welch calls the Spirit the "act of 'community' of Father and Son," pp. 287-8.

[13] *Ibid.*, pp. 289, 222.

[14] *Ibid.*, p. 289.

independent self. This way of reasoning, however, is inconsistent. If it is precluded to accept the social Trinity because it involves the *addition* of incomplete selves, it is surely *equally precluded* to accept Welch's solution, since this involves the *subtraction* of external relations from the one self. These external relations he regards as a mark of creatureliness and hence inapplicable to God. But why should he not equally regard the *incomplete* element in the addition of selves as a mark of creatureliness? What, indeed, Welch has done by sleight of hand is to accept *both* the Trinity of self-consciousness *and* the social Trinity, and to fail to acknowledge his indebtedness to the latter, as well as the essential paradox involved. If we cannot add up incomplete selves, no more can we subtract external relations from the one self. The fact of the matter is, as I have shown in a previous chapter, both symbols are necessary, and only a paradoxical statement can do justice to the truth.

For these reasons, then, we cannot regard the attempt to construct a Trinity on the basis of the structure of revelation, as satisfactory.

CHAPTER VIII

THE TRINITY OF GOD'S ACTIVITY

THERE IS ONE FINAL PATTERN OF TRINITARIAN THINKING WHICH we must consider. It has gained some recent popularity through the writing of a distingushed British novelist, although there have been intimations of it before in the Church's history. It is the attempt to establish the Trinity on the basis of a consideration of the modes of God's activity. It differs from the Trinity of revelation in that the distinctions do not concern different ways in which God reveals himself, but rather different elements in any instance of God's activity. Can a satisfactory Trinity be devised on this principle?

There is a passage in Gregory of Nyssa (*On "Not Three Gods"*), which attempts to make such a series of distinctions. He writes: "The principle of the overseeing or beholding power (i.e., of God: that is, his governing of the universe) is a unity in Father, Son and Holy Spirit. It issues from the Father, as from a spring. It is actualized by the Son; and its grace is perfected by the power of the Holy Spirit." Thus each action of God is seen to have three aspects or elements. Its ultimate origin is to be sought in the Father. Its actualization, whereby it acquires form and significance in the temporal process, is the work of the Son. Its perfection (whatever that may be) is the work of the Spirit. Each individual event is thus a unity, to which each of the Trinity makes his special contribution. "No activity is distinguished among the Persons, as if it were brought to completion individually by each of them, or separately apart from their joint supervision." Not three separate things, but in each instance *one* thing results from their combined and interpenetrating action. Yet the one result can be viewed as the concurrence of their different actions: the Father supplies the source, the Son the actualization, the Spirit the perfection.

Three objections can be raised to such an attempt to distinguish the persons of the Trinity. In the first place, what is being described is God in his relations with the world. Thus there is left unaccounted for the principle by which God is Absolute, beyond, unrelated, and independent of his creation. Such a principle Gregory may well believe more fittingly to be attributed to the divine essence, rather than to any of the persons. It is something they all share, rather than something which distinguishes them. They all participate in the paradox whereby God is both beyond and related. But if this is so, what is the point of distinguishing the "source" from the "actualization"? As we have seen in previous chapters, *this* distinction is really a relic of the old, sharper distinction between God as absolute and God as related. When, after the Arian controversy, this distinction was abandoned in contrasting the persons of the Trinity, there was really no point in retaining this remnant of it. It had meaning only within a context in which the Absolute was regarded as the source of all (and especially of the Son) by virtue of its overflowing nature. Such a view, to be sure, was far from satisfactory; but the retention of just this limited element in it was even more unsatisfactory. When the Father was no longer distinguished from the Son by his absolute character, when (under the biblical influence) he was seen as capable of as *direct* a relation to the world as the Son, the distinction between source and actualizer really lost its point. If the Son brings the world to actuality, he is surely its source. Two terms here are quite unnecessary. The ground which underlies the flux and change of existence, is the ground given to it by its Creator. No sharp contrast between ground and source on the one hand, and actualization on the other, is possible. The real paradox of God as both absolute and related has been transferred to the divine essence. The distinction of Father and Son thus becomes unnecessary.

Even more difficult is the attempt to contrast Son and Spirit in terms of "actualizer" and "perfecter." Why can he who actualizes not also perfect? Wherein lies the deficiency that has to be made good? That Gregory never explains; and, indeed, as we have seen, the place of the Spirit in the Trinity remained ambiguous until Augustine worked out his concept of the uniting bond.

Finally, the attempt to distinguish persons in the Trinity on the basis of discreet aspects of their activity, cannot fail to be an arbitrary procedure. In any event, we can detect an indefinite number of aspects. There is no inner necessity to find three or thirty-three of them. The analysis of reality does not lead to its convenient division into three parts. Any threefoldness we discover in it or superimpose upon it cannot but be arbitrary, however illuminating and useful it may prove for us in understanding it.

The detective-story writer, Dorothy Sayers, has revived this type of thinking in her book, *The Mind of the Maker*. While she states the distinctions somewhat differently than Gregory of Nyssa, they essentially revolve around the same ideas. Because her viewpoint has gained some current popularity, it may be well to analyze it here.

She first put forward her theme in the play *The Zeal of Thy House*. The concluding speech of Michael ran thus:

For every work (*or act*) of creation is threefold, an earthly trinity to match the heavenly.
First: (*not in time, but merely in order of enumeration*) there is the Creative Idea; passionless, timeless, beholding the whole work complete at once, the end in the beginning; and this is the image of the Father.
Second: there is the Creative Energy (*or Activity*) begotten of that Idea, working in time from the beginning to the end, with sweat and passion, being incarnate in the bonds of matter; and this is the image of the Word.
Third: there is the Creative Power, the meaning of the work and its response in the lively soul; and this is the image of the indwelling Spirit.
And these three are one, each equally in itself the whole work, whereof none can exist without other; and this is the image of the Trinity.[1]

What does this imply?

It implies, first, that the distinctions in the Trinity are mirrored in an analysis of man's creative capacity. The image of God in man Dorothy Sayers finds in "the desire and ability to make things" (p. 34). That is how she exegetes Gen. 1:26. "God created" is the clue to the "characteristic common to God and man." If, then, we try to understand what is involved in man's creative activity, we shall have a hint of the nature of the

[1] *The Mind of the Maker*, pp. 37-8.

Trinity. There is an inner connection between God and man as far as they make things.

Two observations may be made about this. For one thing, it is a somewhat dubious exegesis of Gen. 1:26. The image of God is not really to be found in any one aspect of man, but in his total being. The point of the Hebrew story is to set man in his place between the created nature (especially the animals) and God himself. Both his likeness to God and his difference from him are implied; and this part of the story, which comes from "P," the exilic writer, is aimed to offset the more pessimistic note of the earlier writer "J," who stresses that man is made from the dust of the ground (Gen. 2:7). Moreover, in setting man in his proper place in the universe, the exilic author is particularly interested in man's having dominion over the animals. If we are to locate the image in any special feature of man's nature, it would surely be in this: he has dominion over the fish, the birds, the cattle, and so on—which is how the author understands and explains the image in Gen. 1:26. However this may be, the more general notion that man in his total being resembles God, because he is superior to the rest of creation and able to converse with God himself, is what is uppermost in the author's mind.

But the precise exegesis of Genesis is not the central issue. Rather this concerns the question whether trinitarian distinctions are fittingly to be found in the way God does things and is related to his world. The analogy which Miss Sayers draws does not illuminate the central paradox of God in his beyondness and God in his relations with us. It merely concentrates our attention upon this latter theme, and leaves out of account the fundamental question with which trinitarian thinking began. Here, to be sure, Miss Sayers stands in line with the Augustinian development, whereby the direct relation of the Father with the world was established over against the earlier thinking. But this, as we have seen, has bequeathed to all later trinitarian thinking a grave problem. How can Father and Son be properly distinguished? Once the paradoxical duality of absolute transcendence and relatedness is denied as the basic principle of the Trinity, some new principle must be sought. We have seen how this was found in an analysis of God as love, and I have tried to show the difficulty of establishing a Trinity on that basis. Is Miss Sayers any more successful in her attempt to find it in the pattern of creative activity?

The answer must be negative for two reasons. In the first place, her analysis of this activity is incomplete. In the second place, the procedure of applying such analyses of human capacities to the Godhead can never issue in a genuine Trinity.

Miss Sayers thinks of the Creator as a Mind, and finds a threefold structure in the action of this mind as it makes something. This structure, she contends, is not a mere "pictorial analogy" as drawn between man's mind and God's. It is the "integral structure of the universe," and corresponds by "a necessary uniformity of substance, with the nature of God, in whom all that is exists."[2] That is to say, all creative activity reflects an essential pattern, as applicable to God as to man, in a quite literal sense.

Now the question arises whether persons of the Trinity can, in any legitimate sense, be so discovered. When we make something, an endless number of factors is involved. Man is not merely a mind; he creates with his total being. When he writes

[2] *Ibid.*, p. 15.

a book (which is the analogy Miss Sayers most constantly uses), he does a great deal more than the figure of St. Michael informs us in his speech. The writer brings to the task all kinds of experience and tradition, he exercises a great variety of capacities in his human make-up, and his product is the result of his being a member of society. Creative activity, therefore, cannot be neatly organized in the abstractions of idea, energy, and power. These are only three factors in an infinitely complex series of events, capacities, and relationships. Are we to find a person of the Trinity for each of them? Is imagination a "person"; is the unconscious ground from which the idea is born, a "person"? Are the author's background, experiences, social relations, and so on, images of further persons in the Godhead? The fact of the matter is that the analysis of any human activity can never yield a necessary threefoldness. The number is arbitrary, just as is the isolation of a single capacity in man, with which to draw analogies with God. It may be useful and instructive in helping us to understand the nature of creative activity, but there is no way by which we can establish a Trinity from such a procedure. What Miss Sayers has to say about the social implications of her theory, and the uncreative nature of so much modern labor, is very illuminating.[3] So too are her criticisms of poets and writers who fail to achieve a right balance between various aspects of creative activity. But while all this is of value, the value does not stem from the discovery of a real trinitarian structure, but from the abstract isolation of three important elements in the process, and the application of these to various situations. The attempt to superimpose these three abstract categories on the Godhead and

[3] *Ibid.*, pp. 172 ff.

then to claim a Trinity has been discovered, is misleading in the extreme. It is no genuine Trinity, but merely a useful and at times quite penetrating analysis of three aspects of what is involved in making something. But there is no real reason to stop at three, nor is there any validity in isolating idea, energy, and power from a complex process with an indefinite number of terms.

We are surely right to say that if God is creator, he creates in some such way as we do. Were that not so, there would be no point in claiming he is creator. We have, of course, equally to say that he does *not* create in the way we do, since he is God and we are creatures. He creates from nothing, we from something, and so on. Yet when we have analyzed this, or any other aspect of man which in some way resembles God, we have not established a Trinity. We have merely drawn certain analogies between man and God, as far as he is related to us. If he is related to us, there must certainly be such similarities. He is in some way a person, in some way creative, self-aware, loving, and powerful. All these terms, on analysis, can yield three or thirty-three different categories; and they can be shown to interpenetrate each other, and yet to have a relative independence, so that they are all one and yet at the same time three or thirty-three. But no Trinity emerges from this; nor is there a need to call them "persons." They are only aspects of human structure, which can be applied to God in his relations with us, if we also remember the application must be guarded and limited, in order to preserve the right distance between creature and Creator.

To conclude: the Trinity cannot be established by an analysis of God's activity. While this can yield an indefinite number of terms, they are not such that they can be called "persons" in any legitimate sense.

CHAPTER IX

THE MEANING OF THE SYMBOLS, FATHER, SON, AND SPIRIT

We have now pursued our way through the major patterns of trinitarian thinking and have arrived at the conclusion that they all involve arbitrary and unsatisfactory elements. While in each case they deal with issues vital to Christian faith, the solutions they propose do not commend themselves. They are open to question in their concern, for instance, to derive God in his relations from God in his absolute character. The "begetting" of the Son from the Father attempts to solve an essential paradox by a confusing principle of derivation. Equally difficult has been the effort to understand the Trinity in terms of "God is love." While there is value in thinking of God as loving himself and equal value in imagining that God in some way resembles a society, we cannot find a genuine Trinity in either of these concepts. The application to God of the intellectual categories does not help us in understanding the mutual relations of love in Godhead. Nor does the picture of God as a society imply a Trinity. The wedding, moreover, of the old paradox of the Absolute and the Related to the issue of love, only further confuses the question. In other trinities, such as those of revelation and activity, we have found the threeness a highly artificial element. Finally, the symbols themselves of Father, Son, and Spirit are ambiguous, and in many instances are thoroughly unsuitable to denote those principles in the Godhead for which they are used.

We must now ask: is it possible to reconstruct trinitarian doctrine so that these objections, which we have encountered in our study, can be overcome? The answer to this must be in the negative. The trinities we have surveyed confuse rather than illuminate the different problems they have sought to clarify. The terms of these problems do not issue in any neat threeness; the problems themselves are often different problems and have to be treated separately, and the basic symbols are inappropriate to them because of their ambiguous and overlapping nature. The fact that, to preserve essential Christian truths, we must make distinctions in the Godhead, does not mean we can fruitfully join all these contrasts together in a trinitarian pattern. Rather we must deal with each on its own merits and strive to find the most fitting way in which to express the necessary distinctions in each case.

What, then, can the three biblical symbols mean to us? What has our utterance of "Father," "Son," or "Spirit" to do with living Christian faith?

We shall never do better than to start with the basic meaning of the symbols in the New Testament. But we must recognize they overlap, and that they do not form a precise Trinity. We must, however, equally recognize that in each case they give expression to something vital for us to affirm. This, in turn, will lead us to see that the symbols point beyond themselves to basic theological issues. These, for the sake of clarity, will have to be expressed otherwise than by these particular terms. They point to various antinomies in the Godhead and to various distinctions we have to make about God's revelation and his activity. But these contrasts are only confused by continuing to use these symbols for them and by trying to mold them together into a neat trinitarian pattern. Rather they beckon us to other modes of expression to illuminate what is essential for Christian faith and what is implicit in the three dominant ways in which the New Testament speaks to us about God.

When we say "Father," we say something about God as he is made known to us in the biblical revelation. We declare that the one God is he whom we encounter in creation, and in particular in his creation of each of us *individually,* and that he gives each of us his special vocation. He adopts us as sons as we respond to his call; we find in him the loving care and concern we know in the ideal of human parentage; we recognize our subjection to him as a child is willingly subject to the discipline of his parents. We know too, that he is above us. We are not his equals; and though he encounters us as person in dialogue with person, he is our creator. Fatherhood hints at God's transcendence and power, as well as denoting his love and discipline. Yet the term Father cannot fully express God's absolute transcendence, precisely because it is a term of relationship. It points us beyond itself to an essential paradox, which we have to express otherwise. Finally, by "Father" we mean very specifically the Father of our Lord Jesus Christ. We find the true meaning of Father in the intimate relation of self-giving between the heavenly Father and Jesus of Nazareth. Here we see what the ideal relation between Creator and creature must be. Such an ideal relation presupposes, of course, that God himself was at work in Jesus, and not by any effort of a human being could this become real or be made manifest. In the mystery of God this occurs in the incarnate Lord, who does not achieve this status by raising himself out of the ordinary run of mortals by sheer will power. Rather we are forced to say that there God reveals himself to us in terms of a human being and enacts in human history the salvation of men. When, then, we say "Father" we mean our creator, who loves and disciplines us, who calls us to his service, and who makes manifest in Jesus Christ the right relation between man and God.

When we say "Son" we refer to this relation between the heavenly Father and Jesus of Nazareth. It is a relation *within the terms of the incarnation*. It is not a term of dependence, fittingly read back into the Godhead itself. The innumerable difficulties of doing this we have tried to elucidate in previous chapters. We have seen how the term meant a heavenly being, inferior to the Father; then the Logos; and finally the eternal Son, as expressive of God in his relations with the world. But the implicit idea of *deriving* God as unveiled from God as veiled is unwarranted, and has posed all sorts of unnecessary problems for trinitarian thinking. The distinction between God as absolute and God as related, is an essential distinction to make in the Godhead. But the terms Father and Son are altogether unfitting to express it. It is then as a term in reference to the incarnation that Son is appropriate. In the face of Jesus we see both the love of God and the right and ideal relation of self-giving between Creator and creature. A term that belongs to the human nature can no more be read back into the Godhead than the other accidents of the incarnate life. As Son, Jesus is the one who is chosen by God, who responds to his call, even unto the death of the cross; and who is raised in glory. But all this is in reference to the incarnate state, not to the Godhead. That God himself is at work here, I have constantly stressed; but it is God in his relations with us, not God as in some way Son in the Trinity.

When we say "Spirit" we refer to God's dynamic action. We think of God's creative energy as it manifests itself in various ways and as he himself is present in his world. The Spirit is not "it," an effluence from God; but *God himself at work,* creating, re-creating, doing signs and wonders, and sanctifying. Particularly as God makes himself known *within* us and imparts himself to us so that we respond to his call and affirm his revealing acts which confront us, we think of him as Spirit. It would not be right, however, to delimit the work of the Spirit to this internal witness and to God's self-imparting in the act of revelation. The term is broader and refers to him as acting in every possible way. Since, however, the term Son has unique significance with regard to the incarnate life, we are not amiss in thinking primarily of God as *responding* in us to his revelation in Christ, when we speak of the Spirit. It is fundamental to Christian faith that we declare Jesus is Lord, *in the Spirit.* Not by our own resources, or as an equal partner in the act of revelation, do we know God as made manifest in Jesus. Rather is it the work of God himself, who raises us to a new status to respond to his gracious act, and thus anticipates the End of history. The connection of the Spirit with the fulfillment of God's purposes in history I have already indicated in treating the New Testament doctrine. The Spirit is thus God in his dynamic action, and particularly as imparting himself to us. Yet we must recognize the term overlaps that of the "Son." It is by God's Spirit that Jesus fulfills the role he does in the world's redemption; just as it is by his Spirit that God is made known to us as Father. The terms do not denominate precise persons in the Trinity. They are ways of thinking about God from different points of view. And while they point beyond themselves to the necessity of making distinctions in the Godhead, they themselves are *not* the actual distinctions and cannot fittingly express them.

What then are these distinctions? They are manifold, and I need only enumerate a few here.

The most basic one concerns that of contrasting God in his absolute character, or mode of being, from that of God as he is related to his world. Here we meet an antinomy, an essential paradox. There is no way of overcoming it, and we must leave it at that. One mode is not prior to the other; one is not engendered from the other. That is the way God is—absolutely transcendent, single, simple, unveiled, inaccessible, and infinitely above his creation; yet, too, he is related to it. He creates, he manifests his love and enters into the realm of suffering for our redemption. He who is pure joy appropriates the pain born of sin. He who is infinitely removed from creation is the one who creates. He who knows no sin bears the pain of sin. He who is self-sufficient becomes dependent upon his world, since he establishes relationship with it. Everywhere we confront the paradox; nowhere can we resolve it. There is no third term by which to compose it. Yet it is basic to our faith. We can sacrifice neither God's absolute transcendence, nor his intimate relation with the world. To abandon the one is to say he is not really God; to abandon the other is to say he is not the God of our world.

From this there derive many other antinomies of a similar nature. He is joy and suffering; he is rest and motion; he is eternal, yet in time; he is one and yet he is involved in the many. He is unveiled, yet he is veiled. That then is our first antinomy.

There are others which are of a different nature. We say God is love. That means he must express his love in some way whereby he is not dependent upon his creation, since this would destroy his absolute character. We can say he loves himself. But this, while valid, cannot fully express what we mean by love. Hence we must say he is in some sense a society. Only by saying these two apparently contradictory things, as I have shown in a preceding chapter, can we fully indicate what we mean by love. There is no way out of the dilemma. To say only that God loves himself is to introduce an inadequate symbol. Love finds its fulfillment in the mutual relations between persons. The symbol of loneliness is not fully a symbol of love.

We meet another antinomy when we try to think of the way in which God is related to us. He is our ground, and yet he is a person over against us. Here the dilemma of our creatureliness is evident. If he is our ground, how can we be responsible persons? If we owe our very life to him, how can we have any genuine independence and freedom? Yet he encounters us as a person. He says to Adam, "Where are you?" He deals with us as a person addressing another person. And yet our dialogue with him is not a dialogue of equals. If we stand before him, supposedly free and defiant, he says, "Behold your Creator!" From this there stems the anxiety of our existence. God is our ground and yet a person over against us. In our sin we recognize both our guilt and our importance. It is all so contradictory. How can we be guilty, if we are also impotent? Yet the contradiction is solved, not in thought, but in life. We learn the service which is perfect freedom, the truth that only in knowing we are nothing do we become something, and find ourselves able to do things we never dreamed of, by his grace. We become persons as we are bound to him. Such contradictions cannot be solved by thought. We reach ultimate paradoxes. Yet in living them we find new life. That God is our ground and at the same time a person over against us is self-contradictory. But it happens to be true.

We might further analyze such apparent contradictions as that God is wrath and also love. There too we shall never find a solution in our thought. The terms are ultimately self-exclusive; yet they must be applied to God. His wrath against sin does not modify his love. Nor does his love modify his holy wrath against sin. He is both these things; and if he is the God of the Christians, he must be both.

Antinomy, however, is not the only kind of distinction we have to make when we think of God. There are contrasts of a different nature. God reveals himself, we say, in Israel's history as well as in Jesus. He is manifest in some way in creation, and yet in another way in his self-imparting witness. These are all different; and indeed in every act of God there is an unrepeatable and unique element, since it participates in history. We are forced to make innumerable distinctions here, and we cannot of necessity sum them up under any three heads. God is related to his world in a variety of ways, and he manifests himself accordingly. For convenience we can group some together and contrast them with others, but this process will never issue in an essential Trinity. An arbitrary arrangement and analysis is inevitably involved.

My conclusion, then, about the doctrine of the Trinity is that it is an artificial construct. It tries to relate different problems and to fit them into an arbitrary and traditional threeness. It produces confusion rather than clarification; and while the problems with which it deals are real ones, the solutions it offers are not illuminating. It has posed for many Christians dark and mysterious statements, which are ultimately meaningless, because it does not sufficiently discriminate in its use of terms. Christian theology might be aided by abandoning such a procedure and by making clear the inadequacy both of the ambiguous terms and of the threeness into which its doctrines have been traditionally forced. We are confronted in the New Testament with three dominant symbols of God. These we can and should use to express deep Christian concerns. But we should avoid supposing they do not overlap, or that they imply three distinct persons in the Trinity. Rather, on analysis, they point to a variety of distinctions we must make in reference to the Godhead, but which we must express in other ways. Some of these are antinomies, others imply an indefinite number of terms. But there is no necessary threeness in the Godhead.

A CHRISTOLOGICAL NOTE

IN ORDER TO AVOID ALL POSSIBLE MISUNDERSTANDING WITH REGARD TO such expressions as "the man Jesus of Nazareth," which recur throughout these chapters, it may be well to add a brief christological note. It has been constantly stressed that I do not write from a Socinian point of view, but regard the incarnate life of Jesus as the work of God, not primarily of man. Not by man's effort, is salvation achieved; not by the striving of mere human will, can the ideal relation between man and God become manifest and powerful in human history. "God was in Christ reconciling the world to himself" (II Cor. 5:19 R.S.V.).

How can we fittingly express this in theological terms? We have to avoid two dangers. We cannot so state the issue that the human reality of Jesus is undermined. Nor may we so state it that the presence of God in the life and work of the Saviour is compromised. Through Christian history christological views have tended to emphasize one or the other of these two truths: the life of Jesus was a real human life, marked by limitations of knowledge, true temptation, and genuine suffering; and in the life of Jesus, God himself was present, unveiling his mystery and working out in human terms the salvation of man.

Now both these propositions are true, and neither should be compromised. Yet in the ultimate analysis they are self-contradictory. They constitute a paradox which no effort of human thinking can ever overcome. Christological views either accept one part of the paradox and deny the other; or they attempt to compose it, but in actual fact leave it unresolved, so that it still lurks somewhere, hidden in the supposed solution. We may well ask, if we hold these two things to be true, whether it is not better to begin with the paradox and openly espouse it, rather than to seek a solution which cannot but be artificial and unsatisfactory. If Jesus was merely and only a human being, we are at a loss to account for that perfection of self-giving and union of will with his heavenly Father, which is basic to Christian faith. If he was only God clothed in flesh, and not a real, historical *man,* subject to the limitations of humanity and in a genuine sense within the context of the first century of our era, then the temptations become a sham, and the willing obedience to God, which we are called to follow, is no obedience at all. We simply have to say both these things: God entered human life in Jesus of Nazareth; and yet Jesus was an actual human being, subject to the same temptations which confront us, and overcoming them by that union of his will with God's, which we ourselves experience so far as we are victorious.

To find a unity of conception by which to compose this dilemma is foredoomed to failure by the nature of the terms with which we start. Either we end up by saying Jesus was an inspired man, who by the effort of his will achieved a divine status; or we say he was not really a man at all, but God clothed in flesh.

The most famous attempt to solve the problem is that of the Chalcedonian formula: Jesus Christ is one person acknowledged in two natures. The Monophysites were right in objecting to this as in effect hypostatizing the natures, so that two persons resulted. The reality of the incarnation was endangered. Beside God there was *a man.* But the Nestorians were equally right in objecting from the opposite side: the reality of Jesus as a man was endangered. If the ultimate "person" of Jesus Christ is God and not a man, the human nature is unreal. It lacks its most essential element. The doctrine of the *enhypostasia* in Leontius of Byzantium (whereby the humanity finds its center, subject, or person in the Logos), put in the crude but incisive terms of Alcuin, involves this: "In the assumption of the flesh by God, the person perishes, not the nature."

Modern efforts to find a solution have proved no more happy or fruitful than ancient ones. Popularly current is that of Donald Baillie in his *God Was in Christ.* This book is very illuminating in understanding the experience of grace—that in making a right choice a man does not glow with self-esteem, but says, "Not I, but the grace of God, is responsible." The divine side of the experience is logically prior, and we become most fully personal to the extent we are most dependent upon God. But this does not clarify the christological issue in the way Baillie imagines. He does not really explain how it was possible for Jesus to be so fully dependent upon God, that the kind of deep union with God we interruptedly experience in grace, was ever present in him. What has to be accounted for is the fact that Jesus' *response* to God's grace was not interrupted and partial. If we say this was due to an unusual and superabundant presence of grace, then we deny the reality of the humanity. There is no genuine human freedom, and no virtue in the conquest of temptation.

It is not my purpose to examine other views here. I state these things only to show that by speaking of "the man Jesus of Nazareth" in these chapters, I am speaking of one aspect of the reality of the incarnate life. I am not at all denying the *other* truth. But I hold that they must be expressed paradoxically.

READING ABOUT THE TRINITY

SURVEYS

The literature on the doctrine of the Trinity is so enormous that the reader will be advised to begin with a general survey and then to proceed to more detailed works.

Robert S. Franks, *The Doctrine of the Trinity,* (London: Gerald Duckworth & Co., 1953), gives a brief, comprehensive outline of the development of the doctrine. It is clear and readable and carries the story up to the modern day.

The article "Trinity," by William Fulton, in the *Encyclopaedia of Religion and Ethics,* edited by James Hastings, *et. al.* (New York: Charles Scribner's Sons, 1922), vol. 12, pp. 458-62, gives a brief, adequate account.

Claude Welch in his book, *In This Name* (New York: Charles Scribner's Sons, 1952), provides a perceptive and well-informed survey of the doctrine in contemporary theology since Schleiermacher. Every important author is covered, often with incisiveness.

THE CLASSICAL DOCTRINES

A good account of the classical doctrines in brief compass and by various Anglican authors will be found in *Essays on the Trinity and the Incarnation,* edited by A. E. J. Rawlinson (London: Longmans, Green & Co., 1928). The Cappadocians are somewhat misinterpreted, but the level of these essays is otherwise high.

The patristic material is treated with equal penetration and lucidity by G. L. Prestige, in *God in Patristic Thought* (London: W. Heinemann, 1936).

The early development up to the First Council of Nicaea has been covered with characteristic clarity by J. Lebreton, *Historie du dogme de la Trinité,* 2 vols. 7th ed., Paris 1927-28. In Chapter 9 of *A Companion to the Study of St. Augustine,* edited by R. W. Battenhouse (New York:

Oxford University Press, 1955), I have given a summary and critical appraisal of Augustine's great work on the Trinity. The most recent study of the patristic material is by Harry Austry Wolfson, *The Philosophy of the Church Fathers,* vol. 1, Cambridge, Mass., Harvard University Press, 1956. It is thorough and comprehensive, but suffers from too exact schematization. It is especially illuminating on the influence of Philo.

Of the important texts in English translation the following may be mentioned; the first six titles have full introductions and notes:

Tertullian. *Treatise against Praxeas.* Edited with Latin text and translation, by Ernest Evans. Society for Promoting Christian Knowledge, 1948.

Novatian. *Treatise on the Trinity*. Eng. tr. by Herbert Moore. New York: The Macmillan Co., 1919.

Gregory of Nyssa. "On 'Not Three Gods.'" Eng. tr. by Cyril Richardson in *Christology of the Latin Fathers.* Ed. E. R. Hardy. Philadelphia: The Westminster Press, 1954.

Gregory of Nazianzen. "The Theological Orations." Tr. by C. B. Brown and J. E. Swallow. In the same volume.

Augustine. "On the Trinity." Tr. A. W. Haddan. *Nicene and Post-Nicene Fathers* (First Series). Ed. P. Schaff. Buffalo: 1887. Vol. 3.

John of Damascus. "Exposition of the Orthodox Faith." Tr. S. D. F. Salmon. *Nicene and Post Nicene Fathers* (Second Series). Vol. 9, New York: 1899.

Anselm. "Monologium" and "Cur Deus Homo." Tr. S. N. Deane. *St. Anselm* (Religion of Science Library, No. 54). Chicago: Open Court, 1935.

Richard of St. Victor. "On the Trinity." Latin text only available. Migne, *Patrologia Latina.* Vol. 196, cols. 887-992. 1855 (especially Book 3, 1-25).

Thomas Aquinas. *Summa Theologica* (especially Part 1, Questions 27-43). Tr. by the English Dominican Fathers. London: Burns, Oates & Washbourne, Ltd., 1920.

Calvin. *Institutes of the Christian Religion* (Book 1 in vol. I). Tr. John Allen. London: 1838.

Socinus. *The Racovian Catechism.* Tr. Thomas Rees. London: 1818.

ICONOGRAPHY

Lowrie, Walter. *Art in the Early Church.* New York: Pantheon Books, Inc., 1947.

MacHarg, J. B. *Visual Representations of the Trinity*. Cooperstown, New York, A. H. Crist, 1917.
Webber, Frederick R. *Church Symbolism*. Cleveland: J. H. Jansen, 1938.

MODERN WORKS

Claude Welch's survey of modern views, *In This Name* (see p. 153), contains a very comprehensive bibliography, pp. 303-8. We may single out the following titles:

Roman Catholic

Klein, Felix. *The Doctrine of the Trinity*. Tr. Daniel J. Sullivan. New York: P. J. Kenedy & Sons, 1940.
Pohle, Joseph. *The Divine Trinity*. Tr. Arthur Preuss. St. Louis: B. Herder, 1919.

Anglican

Hodgson, Leonard. *The Doctrine of the Trinity*. New York: Charles Scribner's Sons, 1944.
Lowry, Charles W. *The Trinity and Christian Devotion*. New York: Harper Bros., 1946.
Sayers, Dorothy L. *The Mind of the Maker*. London: Methuen & Co., 1942.
Thornton, Lionel S. *The Incarnate Lord*. London: Longmans, Green & Co., 1928.

Protestant

Schleiermacher, Freidrich. "On the Discrepancy between the Sabellian and Athanasian Method of Representing the Doctrine of the Trinity." Tr. Moses Stuart in *The Biblical Repository and Quarterly Observer*, VI, July, 1835. Pp. 1-116.
Barth, Karl. *The Doctrine of the Word of God*. Tr. G. T. Thomson. New York: Charles Scribner's Sons, 1936.
Bartlett, Charles N. *The Triune God*. New York: American Tract Society, 1937.
Brown, William A. *Christian Theology in Outline*. New York: Charles Scribner's Sons, 1906.
Champion, John B. *Personality and the Trinity*. New York: Fleming H. Revell Co., 1935.

INDEX